The Serig Family
in
Wheeling, WV

by
Ross Jennings

The Serig Family in Wheeling, WV

Contents

Acknowledgments

I am grateful to Eli Moses for riding his bike through the Greenwood Cemetery, and to his mother, Amy Moses, for asking about some of the graves there. Without that start, this book would never have happened. A special thank you to Ward Serig for help with his side of the family and for answering many other questions. Thanks also to Margie Mims for help with the Joe Serig side of the family. Finally, thanks to my wife, Karen, mostly for being a Serig, but also for all the help she gave me with this book.

Cover Photo

The Louis August Serig family about 1912, courtesy of Ward Serig.

The family members and the age they turned in 1912 (in parentheses):

    Standing in front: Elbert (4)

    Sitting (left to right): Edith (19); Louis August (41); Amelia (38); Vera (16)

    Standing in back (left to right): Alma (6); Leah (10); Chester (17); Merle (14); Louis Clifford (12); Helen (8)

Chapter I
Overview of the Serig Family in Wheeling

The Objective

This project began in late 2020, during the coronavirus pandemic, when Amy Moses took her young son, Eli, to ride his bike in the safest place near their home, the Greenwood Cemetery in Wheeling, West Virginia. Walking around the cemetery, Amy noticed grave markers with the last name "Serig," her maiden name. She sent a text to her aunt Karen: "These must be relatives, right?" She also sent pictures of markers for two couples, George A. Serig (1871 – 1956) and Maude G. Serig (1877 – 1922) and Charles L. Serig (1901 – 1981) and Wilma V. Serig (1900 – 1983).

Amy's aunt Karen had grown up in Wheeling, and she knew that there were others in Wheeling at that time with the last name of Serig, but her father, Chuck Serig, had always told her they were not relatives.

Karen is my wife, Karen Serig Jennings. I was familiar with genealogy software from researching my own family, so it took only a few minutes on the internet to discover that Karen's family and the "other" Serig family were in fact related.

This discovery left me wondering how two families became so lost from each other that distant relatives living in the same small town, with the same last name, were unaware of their connection. And so began this project. Along the way I found that the first Serigs came to Wheeling more than 180 years ago, and I identified thirty-one of their descendants who still live in the greater Wheeling area. I also discovered that Amy wasn't just lucky to stumble across a Serig grave in the Greenwood Cemetery, there are at least twenty-four such graves there.

This chapter provides a brief summary of the rest of the book, which follows the Serig family from the initial immigrants through succeeding generations to the present, focusing on members of the Serig family who still live in the Wheeling area. With each generation, I drop individuals who did not raise children in the Wheeling area and carry forward to the next generation those who did.

The Immigrant Generation

The Serig family first came to Wheeling in the 1830s when two brothers, Henry E. Serig (1809 – 1851) and Augustus Serig (1812 – 1862) immigrated to the United States from Germany. They may have come together or Augustus may have followed his older brother. Once in Wheeling, they married women who themselves had come from Germany. Henry married Mary Christina Dipple (1813 – 1888), and Augustus married Sophia Henrietta Elizabeth, maiden name unknown, (1820 – 1891). All four of these immigrants appear to be from Hanover, Germany in the state of Lower Saxony, so perhaps they knew each other before coming to the United States. See Chapter II for details on these immigrants.

The Henry Line of the Serig Family

Henry E. Serig had five children, born between 1836 and 1845. Two of these five children did not reach adulthood. See Chapter III for details on this first American-born generation of the Henry line.

The other three children had twenty-seven children between them who were born between 1862 and 1888, Henry's grandchildren and the second generation of the Henry line. Seven of these grandchildren stayed in the Wheeling area to raise their families. Among the others, ten died before they reached adulthood, eight lived to adulthood but did not have children, and two moved from the Wheeling area. See Chapter V for details on this second generation in the Henry line.

The seven members of the second generation who remained in the Wheeling area had thirteen children between them, born between 1897 and 1916. These are Henry's great-grandchildren and the third generation of the Henry line. Six of these thirteen stayed in the Wheeling area to raise their families. Among the others, three had no children and four left the area. See Chapter VII for details on this third generation in the Henry line.

The six members of the third generation who remained in the Wheeling area had twelve children between them, born between 1925 and 1957. These are Henry's 2x great-grandchildren and the fourth generation of the Henry line. Seven of these twelve stayed in the Wheeling area to raise their families. Among the others, two left the area, and I could not find information for the other three. See Chapter IX for details on this fourth generation in the Henry line.[*]

The seven members of the fourth generation who remained in the Wheeling area had eighteen children between them, born between 1950 and 1982. These are Henry's 3x great-grandchildren and the fifth generation of the Henry line. Six of these eighteen stayed in the Wheeling area to raise their families. Ten left the area, and I could not find information for the other two.

The six members of the fifth generation who remained in the Wheeling area had seven children between them, born between 1986 and 1994. These are Henry's 4x great-grandchildren and the sixth generation of the Henry line. All seven stayed in the Wheeling area to raise their families. See Chapter XI for details for both the fifth and sixth generations in the Henry line.

In total, as of April 2021, I was able to identify fourteen descendants of Henry Serig who still live in the Wheeling area. Five are descendants of Henry's son, Louis August Serig (1843-1923), and the other nine are descendants of another of Henry's sons, Albert (1845-1921). Three are from the fourth generation of Henry's descendants, five are from the fifth generation, and six are from the sixth generation.

The Augustus Line of the Serig Family
Augustus Serig had five children, born between 1840 and 1856. Three of these five children did not reach adulthood. See Chapter IV for details on this first American-born generation of the Augustus line

The other two children had nine children between them who were born between 1864 and 1883. These are Augustus' grandchildren and the second generation of the Augustus line. Three of these grandchildren stayed in the Wheeling area to raise their families. Among the others, one died before they reached adulthood, and five lived to adulthood but did not have children. See Chapter VI for details on this second generation in the Augustus line.

---

[*]Throughout the book, 2x great-grandchildren (read as "two times great-grandchildren,") is short for great-great-grandchildren and 3x great-grandchildren is short for great-great-great-grandchildren, and so forth.

The three members of the second generation of the Augustus line who remained in the Wheeling area had eighteen children between them, born between 1884 and 1909. These are Augustus' great-grandchildren and the third generation of the Augustus line. Seven of these eighteen stayed in the Wheeling area to raise their families. Among the others, three died young, three reached adulthood but had no children, and five left the area. See Chapter VIII for details on this third generation in the Augustus line.

The seven members of the third generation who remained in the Wheeling area had twenty-six children between them, born between 1909 and 1940. These are Augustus' 2x great-grandchildren and the fourth generation of the Augustus line. Five of these twenty-six stayed in the Wheeling area to raise their families. Among the others, three died young, five reached adulthood but did not have any children, and thirteen left the area. See Chapter X for details on this fourth generation in the Augustus line.

The five members of the fourth generation who remained in the Wheeling area had thirteen children between them, born between 1938 and 1960. These are Augustus' 3x great-grandchildren and the fifth generation of the Augustus line. Four of these thirteen stayed in the Wheeling area to raise their families. Six left the area, one died young, and I could not find information for the other two. My wife, Karen, is one of the six who left the area.

The four members of the fifth generation who remained in the Wheeling area had eight children between them, born between 1963 and 1986. These are Augustus' 4x great-grandchildren and the sixth generation of the Augustus line. Four of the eight stayed in the Wheeling area to raise their families, and the other four moved elsewhere. My wife's niece, Amy, is one of the four who remained in the Wheeling area.

Nine members of the seventh generation of the Augustus line, born between 2000 and 2016, remain in the Wheeling area. These are Augustus' 5x great-grandchildren. For the most part they are too young to have children. Amy's son, Eli, is one member of this generation.

In total, as of April 2021, I was able to identify seventeen descendants of Augustus Serig who still live in the Wheeling area. All are descendants of Augustus' daughter, Matilda, and all but two are descendants of Matilda's great-grandson, Charles Edward Serig (1923 – 2003). See

Chapter XII for details for the fifth and sixth generations in the Augustus line and these two exceptions. See Chapter XIII for details on Charles Serig and his descendants. Charles had three brothers who left the Wheeling area. The details for those three brothers and their descendants are provided in Chapter XIV. Of the seventeen descendants of Augustus who remain in the Wheeling area, four are from the fifth generation, four are from the sixth generation, and nine are from the seventh generation.

Summary

There are an unknown number of descendants of Henry and Augustus Serig scattered around the country. Imagine that in each generation there had been three children, all of whom remained in Wheeling to raise their families, and who each had three children who also remained in Wheeling, and so forth. After seven generations, two brothers would have produced 4,374 descendants in the Wheeling area. Instead, I found only thirty-one descendants of these two brothers who remained in the Wheeling area. What happened to the rest?

Several trends are obvious over the seven generations covered in this book. First, if fewer children had died before reaching adulthood there would likely be more Serig descendants still in the Wheeling area. Similarly, if more childless individuals had had children there would likely be more Serig descendants still in the Wheeling area.

However, two other trends more than offset the effects of dying young and childless adults. First, families became much smaller over time. The five families from the first America-born generation who stayed in the Wheeling area had an average of more than seven children, but the families from the last three generations had an average of fewer than two children. Also, members of succeeding generations tended to more frequently move away from Wheeling to raise their families. This trend peaked in the third, fourth, and fifth generations when between a quarter and half of the members of those generations moved away from Wheeling.

For the details of who all these people were and how they lived, read on. Some of it may be a little boring, but there some pretty interesting nuggets scattered throughout most of the chapters. If you don't have the patience to read the whole book, be sure to skip to the last chapter and read that one.

Chapter II
The Immigrants

Early Wheeling

The origins of Wheeling date to 1769 when Ebenezer Zane, one of many from east of the Appalachian Mountains looking to settle in the west, arrived at the confluence of Wheeling Creek and the Ohio River. He liked the look of the place, so the next year he returned to stay, bringing his wife and two brothers. A few years later Fort Henry (originally named Fort Fincastle) was built to help protect the growing settlements in the area from Indian attack. The fort later played a role in two battles during the Revolutionary War.

At the end of the war, the area around Wheeling was granted to the state of Virginia, the largest and most populous of the thirteen colonies, and Wheeling was officially established as a town in 1795. The National Road arrived in Wheeling in 1818, linking the town to the Potomac River, and over time, Wheeling became a transportation hub along the Ohio River, lying about 100 miles below Pittsburgh as the river flows, and more than 300 miles above Cincinnati. In 1836, the City of Wheeling was officially incorporated, and by 1840 the population was almost 8,000.

Some of the flavor of early Wheeling can be gleaned from *History of Greater Wheeling and Vicinity: A Chronicle of Progress and a Narrative Account of the Industries, Institutions and People of the City and Tributary Territory* by Charles A. Wingerter, published in 1912.

Wingerter provides a physical description of the city by quoting the Wheeling city directory of 1839:

"The local position of the city is a declivity just sufficient for the rains to elute its surface from accumulating impunities, and to keep it freed from the detention of stagnant water."

"The design of the city appears to have been elicited from the plan of Philadelphia. Although the streets are mostly 60 feet wide, some others vary from 50 to 100 feet, and the alleys are some 16 and some 20 feet wide. The most of them are substantially paved with stone, and run nearly north and south, and are crossed by others at right angles, running from the river eastward, forming squares of appropriate dimensions. Those squares are again equally divided each way, by alleys passing through them, on some of which are erected valuable buildings, and are occupied either as private dwellings, or respectable boarding houses. The sidewalks are permanently paved with brick, and are sufficiently spacious and kept in good order. The buildings are generally composed of brick, though some of stone, and a few of wood. They are mostly from two to three stories high, and substantially built. Many of them are of splendid structure." (page 157)

Various industries for which Wheeling became known began early in its history. Nail making began on a small scale in 1818 and glass making in 1821. The Wheeling Stogie made its appearance in 1840 in a shop run by Mifflin Marsh, who began the business that was later carried on by his son. Wingerter provides this description of business in Wheeling in the late 1830s:

A catalogue of its manufacturies, as they existed in 1835, is printed in Martin's Gazetteer of Virginia, a part of which I shall take the liberty to transcribe. These establishments are "kept in motion by twenty-six steam-engines. The Wheeling iron works roll annually one thousand tons of iron. Besides these, there are four iron foundries, employing seventy hands; four establishments for making steam-engines, also employing seventy hands; five glass-houses; two glass-cutting works employing one hundred and ninety-three hands; three steam flour mills; two steam distilleries; two cotton factories; two paper mills; two steam saw mills; one copperas factory; two soap and tallow chandleries; two tobacco factories; ten bake houses; three printing offices and one book bindery." To these are added a host of operations of a minor sort; such as tailors, wheelwrights, saddlers, silversmiths, painters, rope-makes, etc. etc. I cannot copy the entire list, but the sum of the matter is, "that the whole number of establishments, for the manufacture of domestic goods, amounts to one hundred and thirteen, consuming, yearly, more than one million bushels of coal." Tell me, does not Wheeling deserve to be styled one of the Birminghams of the West? One million bushels of coal! And, perhaps, an equal quantity is consumed for household purposes. Whence comes it? A kind of Providence has stacked away enough of it, within a stone's throw of the fires, there it is wanted, to supply a thousand generations. The hills are full of it, and can never be emptied. It may always be had by the poor for the digging. "Delivered at the factories, the price varies from one to three cents a bushel." Who would desire fuel at a cheaper rate? In Washington, it cost me, last winter, you will remember, thirty-four cents a bushel. (page 156)

Wingerter also quotes from the Wheeling city directory of 1839 to provide a view of the people of Wheeling:

"The citizens of Wheeling are courteous, hospitable, active in business, enterprising, dignified, and intelligent. No idle groups of loungers here occupying the sidewalks beyond business time, to obstruct the passing crowds of the business populace, who in the constant hurry to and fro, with flippant step, are hastening to their various and respective engagements. Here, on the wings of the early morning, come forth the hands of industry, apply the sounds of a hundred different notes, to prosecute with assiduity the unfinished labors of the preceding day. It is amusing, gratifying and instructive to pass along the various workshops on a summer's day, when the windows are thrown up for the admission of air, and view the different mechanical operations carried on among the handicraft trades—while the performance of some of the them is done as quick as presto, others require more the mental exercises.

The rich and the poor meet together, and merit is honored. But few traces here are to be seen of the venalist or the bacchanalian obtruding from their obscene examples, demoralizing effects upon the virtuous order of society. The profligate is without companions, and seeks a country more congenial to his habits of life, while the business man, acting in any sphere of his usefulness, is seconded by the patronage and example of all around him." (page 158)

With these descriptions of Wheeling and its citizens in mind, let's place the Serig family in this setting.

Two Brothers

The early 19th century was a period of high immigration to the United States from Germany, mostly driven by difficult economic times in their home country. Among these immigrants were two brothers from Hanover in lower Saxony, a city about 100 miles south of Hamburg and 180 miles west of Berlin.

Exactly when and with whom the two brothers arrived is not known. The older brother, Henry E. Serig, was born in 1809. He married Mary Christina Dipple, who was born in 1813, but whether they married in Germany or after Henry arrived in Wheeling is not known. Their first child was born in Wheeling in 1836, establishing their presence there, together, by that time. They eventually had five children.

The younger brother, Augustus Serig, was born in 1812. He may or may not have come to Wheeling with his older brother. Augustus married Sophia Henrietta Elizabeth. She commonly went by the name of Elizabeth, but her surname is unknown. Elizabeth's obituary indicates that she came to Wheeling in 1837, and that she and Augustus were married in 1838. Their first child was born in Wheeling in 1840. They also eventually had five children.

Neither of these two families appears in the 1840 census, but by 1850 Henry had established himself as a grocer, and all five of his children had been born and were living with him and Mary. However, less than two years later, in November of 1851, Henry died at the age of 42, leaving his wife and four of their five children. Their daughter, Lusetta, had died a month before her father. They are both buried in the Mount Wood Cemetery in North Wheeling. The cemetery, which is just off National Road about a mile north of downtown Wheeling, was first established by the Woods family in 1831.

In 1850, Augustus and Elizabeth were living with their three oldest children, and a 50-year-old woman, Louisa Serig, likely his older sister. It is unclear when she came to Wheeling, but it appears she never married.

The late 1840s and early 1850s were dynamic years for Wheeling. A free public school system was instituted in 1848-49. A gas works was built and the streets were paved with cobblestone about the same time. Early in 1850 the Wheeling Hospital was incorporated and construction was begun on the McLure Hotel. By 1850, Wheeling's population had grown by 45 percent in the previous decade from 7,885 to 11,510.

One issue that had plagued the city for several decades was the challenge of providing a bridge across the Ohio River to connect Wheeling and West Virginia (then Virginia) with Ohio to the west. In 1837, a wooden bridge was built to connect Wheeling Island with the Ohio side of the river, but there was still no connection between Wheeling Island and Wheeling proper.

In 1847, the state of Virginia approved construction of a suspension bridge across the river, which was finally completed in late 1849. This bridge was not only the first bridge over the Ohio River below Pittsburgh, but it also had the longest single span of any existing bridge at the time, stretching 1,010 feet from tower to tower.

At the next census, in 1860, Augustus was living in South Wheeling with his wife and two of his children and working as a "palero," which means someone working with a shovel as a gardener or a stoker. Less than two years after that, in October of 1862, Augustus died at the age of 50. Augustus left behind his wife and two of his five children. It is likely that the other three had preceded him in death. Augustus is buried in the Mount Zion Cemetery, at 300 Fairmont Avenue in Wheeling, about three miles south of the Mount Wood Cemetery. He is likely one of the first to be burid there.

The two widows lived for many more years.

In the 1865 city directory, Henry's widow, Mary Christina, was living in Wheeling on Water Street "north of the tannery." The "tannery" was most likely the Centre Wheeling Tannery, which was located at approximately 23rd Street between Main and the river. The city directory also listed two of her children as living at the same address, Albert, who was twenty years old, and Louis, who was twenty-two. Albert was working as a blacksmith and Louis as a laborer.

The same 1865 city directory reports that Elizabeth, Augustus' widow, was living at 4th and Chestnut in Wheeling. This is likely current Chapline Street (formerly 4th Street) and 13th (formerly Chestnut). This was about three-quarters of a mile north of her sister-in-law.[*]

In January of 1863, the women were likely at those addresses when the *Wheeling Intelligencer* reported that three drunk men had roamed through Wheeling one night, breaking windows and causing other damage. The article went on to say

> Mrs. Serig testified that on the night in question, a party of men came by her house and picking up a big slop barrel, standing in the yard, threw it through her window into the kitchen, to the great terror and consternation of her unprotected household. She believes it was Franz Schwertferger that did it, for this reason, that he had written her a threatening letter about what he intended to do when he came home from the army at Christmas. Mrs. Serig aroused some of her neighbors at the time, one of whom tracked one of the parties who had done the mischief to the house of Mrs. Roody where Schwertferger boards.

> One witness who knows Schwertferger testified that if he had been drunk enough, he would have thrown anything through anybody's window.

> Mrs. Schwertferger, a very pretty young woman, testified that her husband was in bed before the affair at Mrs. Serig's house. Schwertferger left the city the next morning after the affair and was not on trial.

---

[*] In July of 1873, the City of Wheeling changed the names of many streets. Some named streets became numbered streets more corresponding to a conventional grid system, some numbered streets became named streets, and some streets that had previously changed names along the street's path were given a single name.

It is not clear from the article which Mrs. Serig is being referred to, but it is probably Augustus' widow. She had been a widow for only six months at the time, and was likely living with two minor children, Matilda (17) and Louis (13). Her sister-in-law, Mary Christina, was probably still living with two adult sons.

Henry's widow, Mary Christina, does not appear in the 1870 census. Augustus' widow, Elizabeth, does appear in that census and was living with her son August (21), her daughter Matilda (25), and Matilda's two children, Elizabeth (5) and Caroline (1). August was working in a glass factory. Over the previous several decades Wheeling had developed a robust glass industry with several factories employing nearly 1,000 men.

Mary Christina reappears in the 1880 census, living alone at 41 5th Street in Wheeling, a little north of downtown. At that time, Elizabeth was living at 3723 Jacob Street in Wheeling, south of downtown, about two-and-a-half miles from her sister-in-law. With her were two of her daughter Matilda's children, Elizabeth (15) and Walter (5). Elizabeth, the grandmother, was listed as a confectioner, and Elizabeth, the granddaughter, was working in a confectionary, likely with or for her grandmother.

By the time the two widows died, their families were settled in different parts of Wheeling, Henry's line in the north, and Augustus' line in the south.

Henry's widow, Mary Christina, died in 1888 at the age of 75. She is buried with her husband in the Mount Wood Cemetery.

Augustus' widow, Elizabeth, died three years later, in 1891, at the age of 71. She is buried with her husband in the Mount Zion Cemetery.

Summary

Two brothers from Germany came to Wheeling, West Virginia (then Virginia) in the 1830s, married, and raised their families.

Henry E. (1809 – 1851) and Mary Christina (1813 – 1888) Serig had five children:

- Henry J. (1836 – 1916)
- Lusetta (1839 – 1851)
- William (1842 – 1862)

- Louis August (1843 – 1923)
- Albert (1845 – 1921)

These children are the first American-born generation in the Henry line, and are discussed in the next chapter.

Augustus (1812 – 1862) and Elizabeth (1820 – 1891) Serig also had five children

- Mary (1840 – ?)
- Matilda (1845 – 1892)
- Louis (1846 – ?)
- August W. (1849 – 1922)
- Elizabeth (1856 – ?).

These children are the first American-born generation in the Augustus line, and are discussed in Chapter IV.

Chapter III
First Generation – Henry Line

Henry E. Serig (1809 – 1851) and Mary Christina Dipple (1813 – 1888) were both immigrants to the United States from Germany in the 1830s. As summarized in the family tree below they had five children, all born in Wheeling, the first American-born generation of the Henry line.

Henry E. Serig Family Tree

Henry E. Serig (1809 – 1851) m: Mary Christina Dipple (1813 – 1888)

- Henry J. Serig (1836 – 1916) m: Louisa Maser (1841 – 1928) in 1861
- Lusetta Serig (1839 – 1851)
- William Serig (1842 -1862)
- Louis August Serig (1843 – 1923) m: Sarah Ann Lewellen (1848 – 1927) in 1868
- Arthur Serig (1845 – 1921) m: Sarah Virginia Sykes (1849 – 1944) in 1867

1836 – 1891

Henry J. Serig, Henry E. and Mary Christina Serig's first child, was born on August 30, 1836 in Wheeling. His sister, Lusetta, was born three years later, January 9, 1839, followed in quick succession by William (April 13, 1842), Louis August (October 18, 1843), and Albert (August 21, 1845). The two Henry's can be hard to keep separate, so the father will be referred to as Henry E. and the son will be referred to as Henry J.

Lusetta died October 9, 1851 at the age of twelve. Her father, Henry E., died a month later, on November 9, 1851, perhaps from the same epidemic. Lusetta and her father are both buried in the Mount Wood Cemetery in North Wheeling.

About eleven years later, William died at the age of twenty. He did not marry, and is also buried in the Mount Wood Cemetery. This left three surviving brothers, Henry J., Louis August, and Albert. All three married and between them they had 27 children.

In about 1861, Henry J. married Louisa Maser (1841 – 1928). At the time of their wedding, Henry J. was about twenty-five years old and Louisa was about twenty. Louisa's parents were both born in Germany, so, like Henry J., she was a first generation American-born. Henry J. and

Louisa had eleven children, grandchildren to Henry E. Serig, and part of the second generation of American-born descendants. These children are discussed in more detail in Chapter V.

The Civil War began with the battle of Fort Sumter near Charleston, South Carolina in April 1861. The next month the state of Virginia formally voted to secede from the Union, but the general sentiment in the western part of the state was not to secede. As an example of the role of slavery in the area, in 1860 Ohio County, Wheeling's county, had a white population of 22,196 and only 100 slaves. Over the next two years, the western part of the state, to be called West Virginia, separated from Virginia, and was admitted to the Union as a separate state on June 30, 1863.

In spite of the decision not to follow the rest of Virginia and secede from the Union, West Virginia provided about an equal number of volunteers to both the Union and Confederate forces during the war. One of the many units raised in West Virginia in support of the Union was the 6th West Virginia Infantry Regiment, which was organized on August 13, 1861. Volunteers were recruited from various locations in West Virginia, including Wheeling. Louis August Serig, served in that unit. He enlisted on October 1, 1861, less than three weeks before his eighteenth birthday, and was discharged on November 17, 1864. The regiment spent most of the war guarding the Baltimore & Ohio railroad against Confederate raiders. During the war, the 6th Infantry lost two officers and eight enlisted men killed or mortally wounded in battle and 167 enlisted men dead from disease.

On February 15, 1865, Louis' brother, Albert, enlisted in the 3rd West Virginia Cavalry when he was nineteen years old. The 3rd Cavalry was organized in December of 1961, and saw action in many battles, including the second battle at Bull Run, and the battle of Gettysburg. Albert joined the unit just in time for the battle that ended the war, Lee's surrender at Appomattox Court House on April 9, 1865. During the war, the 3rd Calvary lost six officers and forty enlisted men killed or mortally wounded in battle and 136 enlisted men dead from disease.

After the war, in 1867, Albert married Sarah Virginia Sykes (1849 – 1944). Sarah was born and raised in Wheeling. At the time of their wedding, Albert was about twenty-two years old and Sarah was about eighteen. Albert and Sarah had six children, part of the second generation of descendants of Henry E. Serig. They are discussed in Chapter V.

The next year, in 1868, Albert's older brother, Louis, married Sarah Ann Lewellen (1848 – 1927). Sarah was born near Pittsburgh, Pennsylvania, and at the time of the 1860 census she was eleven years old and living there with her family. Her father was born in Virginia and her mother was born in Pennsylvania. During the Civil War Sarah's father, Thomas Lewellen, served with the 3rd Pennsylvania Heavy Artillery Regiment from February 14, 1864 to November 9, 1865. At the time of their wedding, Louis was twenty-four years old and Sarah Ann was twenty. Louis and Sarah had ten children, part of the second generation of descendants of Henry E. Serig. They are discussed in Chapter V.

The 1870 census shows Louis (26), living in Wheeling with his wife, Sarah (called Annie in the census, 22), and their daughter Mary (11 months). Louis had $1,500 of real estate and $300 of personal property. His younger brother, Albert (24), was living in Triadelphia, about seven miles east of Wheeling, with his wife Sarah (19) and their son William (1). Albert did not own any real estate and had $100 of personal property. Both brothers were working in a rolling mill.

A number of Henry J. Serig's children did not survive to adulthood. On August 23, 1872 *The Wheeling Daily Intelligencer* reported that Eddie Serig (his full name is Charles Edward Serig), the son of Henry J. and Louisa Serig, had died at the age of 9 months and 10 days. The funeral was to take place at the parent's residence on Main Street. He is buried in the Mount Wood Cemetery in North Wheeling.

Seven years later to the day, on August 23, 1879, *The Wheeling Daily Intelligencer* reported that Lusetta Serig, the youngest daughter of Henry J. and Louisa Serig, had passed away at the age of five weeks and two days. She had the same name as her aunt, who herself had died as a child. The funeral was to be held at her parent's home at 95 Main Street. She is also buried in the Mount Wood Cemetery in North Wheeling.

At the time of the 1880 census, Louis (34) was living at 430 Coal Street in Wheeling with his wife, Annie (31), and their four children, and working as a heater, someone who assists a forger in an iron works.

The same census shows that Albert (34) had relocated to Union Township in Marshall County, south of Wheeling. He was living with his wife Sarah (30) and their four children, and working as a blacksmith.

For some reason their older brother, Henry J. Serig, does not appear in a Federal census again until 1900. However, he does appear in several city directories.

During the early 1880s both Louis and Henry J. were named in a law suit as stockholders of the bankrupt Mingo Junction Iron Works, an Ohio corporation. Wheeling citizens had invested about $140,000 in the bankrupt company and Nimick & Co., probably creditors of the bankrupt company, were suing to get their money back. Mingo Junction had debts of nearly $300,000. In 1884 the West Virginia Supreme Court decided that Ohio law, not West Virginia law, provided Nimick with a path forward. On September 29, 1887 *The Wheeling Daily Intelligencer* reported that Louis Serig was ordered to pay $750 to the special receiver in the Mingo case.

In 1887, Albert applied for a disability pension based on his Civil War service, and his wife, Sarah, applied for a widow's pension in 1921, the year in which Albert died.

In the late 1880s, Wheeling built a new crematory to burn the city's garbage and night soil, and in January of 1887 Henry J. Serig was selected as the facility's first superintendent.

On March 2, 1887, *The Daily Register* reported the following regarding the new crematory:

> There can no longer be a doubt of the entire success of the crematory, as far as its capacity to destroy the objectionable features of night soil, garbage and miscellaneous refuse of all kinds is concerned. Monday's experiment demonstrated that fact, and yesterday's test clinched the matter on the under side. . .

> After infinite trouble about twenty barrels of what was supposed to be night soil was transported to the crematory during Monday night, the work taking up most of the time until daylight yesterday morning, as it was found impossible to haul more than three barrels at a time up the heavy road to the furnace. The fire had been kept going all night by Mr. Serig and by noon the furnace was glowing with an intense heat, sufficient to melt steel or any other metal in a very short time. Quite a number of interested gentlemen were on the ground early in the day,

some of the more enthusiastic bringing their dinners with them, and eating at an impromptu table at the south end of the furnace. . .

Four months later, following a series of delays, the crematory was still not operational. However, it eventually became operational, and in January 1888 Henry J. Serig, as keeper of the crematory, reported to the city council that during the month of December the crematory consumed sixty-one loads of garbage, 126 barrels and boxes, five dogs, forty-three loads of contents of ash vaults, and twenty-six barrels of night soil.

At the end of the next month, it was announced that the "new" crematory would be temporarily shut down for repairs.

> . . . Keeper Serig reported to the Health Committee that the state of affairs was such that it was absolutely necessary to make repairs before much more would could be done in the old rattle trap. The committee groaned and again protested against the luck that had placed them in charge of the affair and then inquired what had to be done. Mr. Serig explained that the brick checker work would probably have to be torn out and reset and a new bottom put in. As to the cost, there was no telling what it would amount to; the committee at a previous meeting had in marking up its annual estimate, allowed $150 for the work. As it was something that had to be done or else abandon the crematory, the necessary repairs were ordered.

A month later, the crematory was back in service, but a severe wind damaged the building, which sat atop Wheeling Hill.

In the midst of these troubles with the crematory, Henry E. Serig's widow died. Her obituary appeared in *The Wheeling Daily Intelligencer* on February 10, 1888, and read as follows:

> The funeral of Mrs. Christina Serig took place yesterday forenoon from the residence of her son, Mr. Henry Serig, superintendent of the city crematory, on North Main Street, and was largely attended. Rev. E. H. Dornblaser, of the English Lutheran Church, and Rev. P. Ziegelmeier, of Zion's German Lutheran Church, officiated and the services were very impressive. The internment was in Mount Wood Cemetery. Mrs. Serig was an old resident, and beloved by all who knew her, and the family have the warm sympathy of a wide circle of friends.

About eighteen months later, this story appeared in *The Wheeling Daily Intelligencer* in June of 1889:

> A horse belonging to Seibert, the ice man, died yesterday. Keeper Serig of the crematory, complains that it was hauled to the top of the hill and left there when the crematory was cold for repairs. He objects to having

to handle dead horses without assistance from those who bring them up or from others.

The city budget for 1890, as reported in *The Wheeling Intelligencer* in January of 1890, showed $729 for Henry Serig as Keeper of the Crematory and $427 for Louis Serig, Henry's 47-year-old younger brother, as a laborer at the Crematory. A year later, in January of 1891, Michael Dunn was selected to replace Henry Serig as Keeper of the Crematory. Four years later, in January of 1895, Henry's brother, Louis, was selected as superintendent of the crematory.

The local newspapers also reported miscellaneous family news. For example, it was reported in 1898 that Cora Serig, Louis' youngest daughter, won second prize for composition by a girl pupil under twelve years. She was ten years old at the time. Earlier that year, this item appeared in *The Wheeling Intelligencer* on January 19, 1898:

> Mrs. Albert Serig was the lucky person in the bean guessing contest at the Indian doctor's farewell performance. She guessed the correct number, 602, and another lady also guessed this number, but in the draw to settle the contest, Mrs. Serig was successful, winning a handsome silver tea set.

Local newspapers also reported land transactions, including many by the Serig family. For example,

In 1868, *The Wheeling Daily Register* reported on April 13, that John Bates and his wife sold to Louis Serig a lot with 33 feet of frontage on Coal Street (now Kenny) in North Wheeling for $1,200. Louis would have been about twenty-five years old at the time.

The Wheeling Daily Intelligencer reported on June 6, 1874 that Lewis L. Smallwood and his wife sold the southern 25 feet of lot No. 1, Bushfield & McMechen's addition to Albert Serig. No price was reported. Albert would have been about twenty-nine years old at the time.

The Wheeling Daily Intelligencer reported on August 8, 1874 that John A. A. E. Elliott and his wife sold 38 feet of lot No. 61 on Main Street in North Wheeling to Henry Serig for $2,700.

In 1880, Albert Serig purchased lot No, 50 in section D of the Mount Wood Cemetery for $30. In 1881, his older brother, Louis, purchased lot No. 108 in section C of the Mount Wood Cemetery for $50.

In January 1886, Louis Serig and his wife sold a lot on the east line of Coal Street (now Kenny) to Henri Claus for $900.

In October 1887 Albert Serig sold the east half of lot No. 212 in section 7 of the Mount Wood cemetery to Martin Kernel for $12.

In April of 1900 Mary and James McCauliff sold to Louis A. Serig lot 29, in square 19 of the Sprigg & Ritchie's addition for $1,725.

Also, as reported in the local newspapers, the Serigs, especially Henry J., were active in local civic affairs. For example, in February of 1865 *The Wheeling Daily Register* reported that Henry J. Serig was the secretary of the organizing committee for the upcoming Fireman's Parade in honor of George Washington's birthday on February 22.

In February of 1868, *The Wheeling Daily Intelligencer* reported that the Wheeling Iron and Nail Works Company was calling a meeting of the stockholders. Henry J. Serig was among the thirteen signees, apparently a member of the board of directors.

Both Henry J. and his younger brother, Louis, were involved in Republican politics at the local and state level for many years. In January 1877, and again in 1879, Henry J. was a delegate to the local Republican convention.

Seven years later, the *Wheeling Sunday Register* reported in April 1884 that Louis was elected as a delegate to the local Republican convention, and two months later, the same newspaper reported that Henry J. was selected as a delegate to the Republican state convention.

In September 1886 Henry J. was selected as the Republican candidate for county commissioner from the Washington District, but he narrowly lost in the general election.

In January of 1888 the Republican party organized local clubs. The club in the Washington District was called the Washington District Garfield Guards, and Henry J. Serig was selected as Third Vice President. That same year, Henry J. was again nominated as the Republican candidate for county commissioner from the Washington District, but he again lost in the general election.

1890 – 1915

In 1892 Henry J. Serig was operating a grocery at 93 Main and resided next door at 95 Main. He was still operating the grocery and living at 95 main Street in 1903.

In late January of 1892 *The Wheeling Daily Intelligencer* reported the following:

> Night before last burglars attempted to gain an entrance into Serig's grocery, on North Main street, by prying open the door with a jimmy, but there happened to be two boards leaning against the door and in their operations the thieves knocked them down, and the noise thus made frightened them off and they left without accomplishing their purpose.

> The fellow who attempted to break into the house has been captured, Officer Seally had obtained the description of a man who had been seen loafing around Serig's house, and was walking along Main street yesterday evening about 8 o'clock in company with Officer Fahey. They saw a fellow answering the description and both nailed him. On the way to the lockup the man wilted, acknowledged having attempted to break into Serig's, confessed to having stolen a pair of gloves on the South Side and owned up to have served a year's workhouse sentence in Pittsburgh for stealing a horse. He was so glib with his confidences that some of the police think he is crazy. A cold chisel about a foot long was found on his person. He gave his name as Thomas Stikles.

As further evidence of Henry's stature in the community, in January of 1898, *The Wheeling Daily Intelligencer* reported the semi-annual statement of the Mutual Savings Bank of which Henry J. Serig was a member of the board of trustees. Henry later served as vice president of the bank. This bank had been founded in 1887 and was the only cooperative savings bank in West Virginia.

By 1910, Henry J. was 73 years old and had retired, but he was still living at 95 North Main Street in Wheeling. With him were with his wife, Louisa (69), and the following children: Lizzie (38); Cloda (35); and Carl (25). Lizzie was a seamstress, Cloda was not working, and Carl seems to have taken over the grocery.

Based on city directories, Louis was living at 218 Coal Street in Wheeling throughout the 1890s. After Wheeling's widespread changing of street names in 1873, much of what was Coal Street became Kenny Street. Louis' occupation was variously listed as a tube worker or heater.

218 Coal Street was about two-tenths of a mile from Henry's house on Main Street in North Wheeling.

In the 1900 census, Louis (56); was still living at 218 Coal Street with his wife Sarah (52), her sister, Martha Lewellen (43), and the following children: Mary (dress maker and 31); Martha (stenographer and 26); Frank (potter and 24); Harry (glass worker and 17); Chester (student and 14); and Cora (student and 12).

In 1910, Louis (66) was working as a fireman at the water works, and still living at 218 Coal Street with his wife Sarah (62), her sister, Martha Lewellen (56), and the following children: Mary (dress maker and 40); Frank (laborer at glass works and 35); Chester (salesman and 24); and Cora (not working and 22).

In 1900, Albert (54) was living at 4804 Main in Benwood, about five miles down the river from Wheeling, with his wife Sarah (50) and their children, Nora (29), Sarah (22), and Albert (19). Albert the father was working as a blacksmith, and Albert the son was working as a tube worker. All of the women were listed as doing housework.

In 1910, Albert (64) was living in Richland, a district in Ohio County, with his wife Sarah (60) and their daughter Nora (40), and he was working as a blacksmith in a rolling mill.

After 1915

Henry J. Serig died on November 21, 1916 in Wheeling, at the age of 80. The 1920 census shows his widow, Louisa (76), living at 95 North Main Street in Wheeling with two of their children, Elizabeth (50) and Cloda (40); and a boarder, Margret Carroll (57). Elizabeth was a seamstress, and Margret was a tobacco packer.

Louisa lived for another twelve years after Henry's death. She died on December 12, 1928 in Wheeling at the age of 87. Both Henry and Louisa are buried in the Mount Wood Cemetery.

Henry's brother, Louis, was admitted to a veteran's home (based on his service during the Civil War) in Dayton, Ohio on November 3, 1917, suffering from defective hearing, chronic constipation, arteriosclerosis, and myocarditis. He left the home on December 19, 1917.

In the 1920 census, Louis (76) was still living at 218 Coal Street with his wife Sarah (72), her sister, Martha Lewellen (66), and two of their children, Frank (43) who was working as a laborer at a cabin factory, and Cora (22), who was working as a sales lady at a dry goods store.

Three years earlier, on April 5, 1917, *The Wheeling Intelligencer* had a full-page advertisement from the Geo Stifel Co., a dry goods store that grew to be a prominent department store, that read as follows:

> **To the Citizens of Wheeling**: At this time of crisis in the affairs of the Nation, when at any moment we may find ourselves forced into a war that we have steadfastly sought to avoid, it is fitting that American men and women should have the opportunity, as unquestionably they have the will, to give assurance of their loyal support to the Government in its measures to uphold American rights and protect the lives of American citizens.

> It may be said that public approval of protective measures is to be taken for granted. But what is understood at home may easily be misunderstood abroad. The great stir raised by small but energetic groups whose cry is surrender, is calculated to encourage new aggressions upon our National rights. . . It is now time that the great majority of Americans should speak, and that their meaning should be unmistakable.

> To that end the Wheeling Commercial Association, will afford to the citizens of Wheeling an opportunity for individual expressions through a declaration of loyalty and support to our Government, addressed to the President of the United States. This declaration, which appears below, will be available for signature at accessible places throughout the city.

The Declaration read as follows:

> **To the President of the United States**: As an American, faithful to American ideals of justice, liberty and humanity, and confident that the Government has exerted its most earnest efforts to keep us at peace with the world, I hereby declare my absolute and unconditional loyalty to the Government of the United States and pledge my support to you in protecting American rights against unlawful violence upon land and sea, in guarding the Nation against hostile attacks, and in upholding international right.

The declaration was followed by the signatures of all of the staff of the Geo E. Stifel Co. store present on April 4th, 1917, which included Cora Serig. President Wilson had called for a declaration of war against Germany three days before this advertisement appeared in the newspaper, and Congress declared war on Germany the day after this advertisement appeared in the newspaper.

In addition to an expression of support for the country, Stifel may have also had a business reason for this advertisement. There was growing anti-German sentiment in the country as the U.S. came closer to war with Germany, and Stifel as an American-born son of German immigrants may have felt exposed to this prejudice.

Two-and-a-half years later, the war had been over for almost a year and life had returned to normal. This social item appeared in *The Wheeling Intelligencer* on October 31, 1919:

> Mr. and Mrs. H. A. Albright entertained with a delightful affair last evening complementary to their visitors, Miss Gressa Maser and Miss Tessie Dinsmore of Parsons, Kansas. The affair was a dinner party of charming appointments given at Wayman's Inn at Bethel. The party motored to the country inn, and following the serving of dinner, a pleasant evening of varied social pastimes was enjoyed.

A list of the guests attending followed, which included Mr. and Mrs. Carl Serig, Mr. and Mrs. H. J. Serig, Miss Elizabeth Serig, Miss Cloda Serig, and Mrs. Laura Bell, who together made up nearly the entire party. H. J. Serig is Herman Jacob Serig, whose mother was Louisa Maser, and hence the connection to the visiting Miss Maser. Carl Serig, Elizabeth Serig, Cloda Serig, and Laura Bell were Herman's siblings.

Louis August Serig died on December 18, 1923, in Wheeling, at the age of 80. Louis' widow, Sarah, lived for four more years, until her death on May 15, 1927, at the age of 79. Both Louis and Sarah are buried in the Mount Wood Cemetery.

In 1920, Albert (44) was living at 140 Warwood Avenue in Richland, a district of Ohio County, with his wife Sarah (70) and their daughter Nora (50). None of them were working.

Albert died on August 19, 1921, two days short of his 76th birthday. Albert's widow, Sarah, lived for many more years as the last survivor of this generation of the Henry line, albeit by marriage.

In 1928, Sarah was living at 704 Warwood Avenue in Wheeling, and she was at the same address in 1940, living with a servant, Stella Mobley (54). Sarah died on January 29, 1944 at the age of 95. Both Albert and Sarah are buried in the Mount Wood Cemetery.

Summary

Henry E. (1809 – 1851) and Mary Christina (1813 – 1888) Serig, came to Wheeling, West Virginia (then Virginia) from Germany in the 1830s, had five children. Although two of these children likely died before reaching adulthood, the other three children together produced twenty-seven grandchildren for Henry E. Serig. His eldest son, Henry J., had eleven children, Louis August had ten children, and Albert had six children. These twenty-seven grandchildren of Henry E. Serig, the second American-born generation in the Henry line, are discussed in Chapter V.

The next chapter discusses the first American-born generation of the Augustus line. For convenience, the following table summarizes the first generation for both the Henry line and the Augustus line.

The First American-Born Generation				
The Henry Line			**The Augustus Line**	
Henry E. Serig (1809-1851) and Mary Christina Dippple (1813-1888)			Augustus Serig (1812-1862) and Sophia Henrietta Elizabeth ? (1820-1891)	
Henry J.	(1836 – 1916)		Mary	(1840 – ?)
Lusetta	(1839 – 1851)		Matilda	(1845 – 1892)
William	(1842 – 1862)		Louis	(1846 – ?)
Louis August	(1843 – 1923)		August William	(1849 – 1922)
Albert	(1845 – 1921)		Elizabeth	(1856 – ?)

Chapter IV
First Generation – Augustus Line

Augustus Serig (1812 – 1862) and Sophia Mary Elizabeth (1813 – 1888) were married in about 1839. Sophia's last name is unknown, but she generally went by the name of Elizabeth. The couple had five children, all born in Wheeling over the 16 years between 1840 and 1856. These five children are the first American-born generation of the Augustus line, and are summarized in the family tree below.

Augustus Serig Family Tree

Augustus Serig (1812 – 1862) m: Sophia Mary Elizabeth (1813 – 1888) about 1839.

- Mary Serig (1840 – ?)
- Matilda Serig (1845 – 1892) m: Louis Harding (1840 – 1869) in 1867
- Louis Serig (1846 – ?)
- August William Serig (1849 – 1922) m: Mary Cook (1851 – 1934) about 1873
- Elizabeth Serig (1856 – ?)

<u>1840 – 1890</u>

Mary Serig, Augustus' and Elizabeth's first child, was born in Wheeling in 1840. She was followed by Matilda on March 30, 1845, and Louis in 1846. Their fourth child, August William, was born on November 17, 1849, and finally Elizabeth was born on January 5, 1856.

In the 1850 census the family included three of the four children who were born before that time, Mary (10), Matilda (5), and August William (0). Louis was not listed. He would have been about four years old, suggesting that he may have died before the census.

In the 1860 census the family was living in South Wheeling and the only children at home were Mary (20) and August (10). Matilda would have been fifteen, and apparently already out of the house. Elizabeth was not listed. She would have been about four years old, suggesting that she may have died before the census.

There is no record of Mary after the 1860 census, leaving only Matilda and her younger brother, August.

Matilda Serig

The story of Matilda is unusual for the time. Her first child, Elizabeth (1864 – 1943), was born on August 7, 1864, apparently out of wedlock, when Matilda was nineteen. About three years later, Matilda married Louis Harding on June 30, 1867. According to the 1868 Wheeling City Directory, Louis Harding was living in Wheeling on 4th between Walnut and Chestnut. This is likely current Chapline Street (formerly 4th Street), between 12th (formerly Walnut) and 13th (formerly Chestnut). At the time, Louis was working as a huckster (door-to-door salesman), and presumably living with Matilda and her young daughter, Elizabeth. Spouses and minor children were not included in the city directory.

Matilda's second child, Caroline (1868 – 1954), was born on February 9, 1868, just over seven months after her marriage to Louis Harding, so she may have been pregnant at the time of their marriage.

Louis' last name is variously given in historical records as "Harding" and "Harting." It appears that he died in January 1869—a Louis Harting who died at that time is buried in the Mount Zion Cemetery. This is the cemetery generally used by the Augustus line of the Serig family.

The 1870 census shows Matilda living in Wheeling with her mother, her younger brother, August William (20), and her two daughters, Elizabeth (6) and Caroline (2). Matilda's name in the census, and the names of her daughters, were all given as Serig. August was working in a glass factory. That year, the census did not include street addresses or marital status.

In the 1872 Wheeling City Directory, Matilda Harding is listed as a widow, living on the west side of 4th between Walnut and Chestnut, the same address as given for Louis in the 1868 city directory. Her next-door neighbor from the 1870 census, the brewer Henry Knoke, is also shown in the 1872 directory as living on 4th between Walnut and Chestnut indicating that she had also been at this address in 1870.

Thus, it seems pretty certain that Louis Harding died in 1869, after only about eighteen months of marriage, leaving behind his widow, Matilda, who was not quite twenty-four years old, with two young daughters, Elizabeth (4) and Caroline (not quite one year old). At the time of his death, the family was living on 4th between Chestnut and Walnut, where they continued for at least the next three years.

Matilda's third child, Louis August (1871 – 1946), was born on February 17, 1871, two years after Louis Harding's death. The child's first and middle names were possibly after her late husband (Louis) and her brother (August). Matilda does not seem to have been married at the time, and she gave the child her maiden name, Serig, as the surname. But who was his father?

Oddly, on Louis' death record in 1946 his father is listed as August Serig, his uncle. Of course, this is possible, but I think it is not likely. The death certificate lacks credibility in several ways. It lists Matilda as his mother, but provides no last name, even though she was a Serig. Also, both August and Matilda are described as born in Germany, even though both were born in Wheeling. The informant was Louis Clifford Serig, Louis August Serig's son. He was born in 1900, about eight years after the death of Matilda, his grandmother. His uncle, August William lived until Louis Clifford was about 22. Did he think this man was actually his grandfather, not his great uncle? If so, what did he think about Walter Harding (see below), his other great uncle. Perhaps Louis Clifford just didn't know much about the family history, especially its darker moments, which seems the most likely. Still, it is possible that Louis' father was his uncle. We'll never know.

Matilda's fourth child, Walter Albert Harding (1876 – 1940), was born on August 21, 1876. Matilda still seemed to be unmarried. Why Louis August was named a Serig, and Walter Albert was named a Harding is unknown. His death certificate in 1940 lists Matilda Serig as his mother and Louis Harding as his father, even though Louis Harding had been dead for about seven years at the time of his birth. The informant was listed as his niece, Carrie Allen, the daughter of Matilda's last child, Caroline. Carrie's grandfather was in fact Louis Harding, so maybe she just assumed he was the father of her just-deceased uncle, Walter Harding. What any of Matilda's children knew about their parentage, and what they told their children, remains a mystery.

After four children under what must have been somewhat scandalous circumstances for the time, Matilda's life did not get any simpler. A little over two years later, on December 24, 1878, the following article appeared in *The Wheeling Intelligencer*:

Geo. Baum, who was a member of the police force for a number of years, under City Sergeants Davis and Ripley, was before the police court yesterday morning on a charge of committing adultery with Mrs. Serig who resides with her mother at No. 3723 Jacob Street, South Wheeling. Baum was arrested by Officer Asmus, at Mrs. Serig's house, about 2 o'clock Sunday morning. Messers. Alfred Caldwell and B. B. Dovener appeared for the prisoner, and asked for a continuance to this morning, which was granted.

It is claimed by the defendant's counsel that Asmus broke in the door of Mrs. Serig's house at the time the arrest was made, and declared Baum under arrest without showing a warrant; that defendant did not know what charge had been brought against him until he saw the warrant, for the first time, at the police court; and that he was lodged in the lockup and kept there until Sunday, although he sent a friend with $50 to police headquarters at the city building, as a deposit to insure his appearance for a hearing, the proffered security being refused. In brief the defendant claims that the officer, without a warrant, broke open the door of a private residence and took therefrom a citizen without any authority whatever; that double the amount of bail usually required was proffered and refused, when it is well known that the custom of receiving bail is one of long standing; and that no warrant was issued until Monday morning.

As is pretty generally known, no love exists between Asmus and Baum, some animosity having grown up between them on account of the former superseding the latter on the police force; and whether Baum be innocent or guilty, of the offense with which he stands charged, one thing seems clear, that is that the officer was not actuated solely and exclusively by a burning desire to perform his duty in making this arrest. It is the opinion of many citizens of South Wheeling that Baum's arrest by Asmus and Paul Heller, the latter having been brought along by the officer to be conveniently deputized to assist in handling the burly burgomaster in case he should not tamely submit to being dragged off to durance vile, smacks a good deal of malice and spite work on the part of the two gentlemen who so suddenly developed an extraordinary desire to enforce the ordinances of the city.

Mrs. Serig in the article above must be Matilda, who apparently was living with her mother, Augustus' widow, Elizabeth (60). About eighteen months after this incident, in the (June) 1880 census, Matilda's mother is shown as living at 3723 Jacob Street with two of her grandchildren, Elizabeth (15) and Walter (5). I cannot find Matilda or her other two children, Caroline (12) and Louis (9), in the 1880 census.

The following story may explain her absence from the census. On May 7, 1881, the following article in its entirety appeared in *The Daily Register*:

There was trouble in a Smith family yesterday, and a reporter had to be detailed to follow the case around among different justice shops. The case came from South Wheeling, and was very interesting in some particulars. The story, as learned is this:

Jonathan Smith as he was named, but John Smith as he is called, came home from work Thursday night and found, as he claims, that his wife had moved some of the household goods into her mother's house, it being a double house. He broke up the stove with a flat-iron; says the women called him names. They say he threatened to kill them and locked the house up. Both parties looked for police and hunted the Squires' offices.

Smith has been married three times. He married his second wife while his first wife was still living, and served a term in the Ohio penitentiary for playing Mormon. When he got out, he was free of both wives, and proceeded to hunt up another. About a year ago, he found her (his present wife) a widow living with her mother, who has some of this world's goods and a daughter, a buxom lass of 14, in Guernsey County Ohio.

The wedding took place and they came to Wheeling. She found out that he had been in prison and accordingly sued for a divorce. He promised, however, to leave if she would furnish the capital. This she did, and he left, the divorce suit still pending in Circuit Court of this county. Sometime after she received a note saying that her husband had been run over and killed on the T. V. road and if $20 was sent his remains would be forwarded. The divorce suit was withdrawn and a letter sent ordering the remains to be send C. O. D.—but they came not; a few days after, however, Jonathan or John turned up safe, sound and sheepish.

He induced the woman to take him back, but things have not been pleasant and culminated in Thursday night's blowout.

Yesterday's program was as follows: in the morning, Smith instituted suit against Matilda, his wife, before Squire Felber for unlawful detention of property. It was settled by the costs being placed on him, and Matilda returning the few goods she had removed into her mother's half of the house, and about whose proprietorship there was no doubt.

At 4 o'clock P.M., before the same justice, John complained against Matilda, charging her with bad and angry words, to the disturbance of the peace. She was fined $1 and costs.

At 5 o'clock Squire Philips' office was the objective point. John had here sworn out a warrant against Elizabeth Serig, his wife's mother, and Carrie Hardin, his step daughter, charging them with tumult and disorder. A long story was rehashed and the cases dismisses at the cost to the complainant. In all the cases Arnett appeared for Smith and

Dovener for the women. It was fun to see the counsel chin each other occasionally.

After the Philips trials a constable from Squire Felber took charge of Smith to look after his costs and there was some talk of a commitment.

The Wheeling City Directory for 1882 shows that Matilda (37) was widowed and living at 3735 Eoff Street in Wheeling with her widowed mother (62) and her daughter Elizabeth (18). This house was about two miles south of their previous address on 4th Street. Minor children were not separately listed in these city directories, so the other children Caroline (14), Louis (11), and Walter (6), may have been living with them also.

The Wheeling City Directory of 1884 shows only Mrs. Elizabeth Serig (widow) and her granddaughter Lizzie (Elizabeth) living at 3735 Eoff Street. It could be that Louis and Walter, as minor children not listed, were also living there. Caroline was married that year, and may or may not have been living with her grandmother at the time the city directory was compiled. I cannot find a record of where Matilda was at that time.

The Wheeling City Directory of 1886 shows that Matilda (widow), Lizzie and Louis Harding are all boarding at 3735 Eoff Street, with Elizabeth Serig (widow). Lizzie (Elizabeth) was about 22 years old, and Louis was about 16, perhaps old enough for a male to be listed separately. Lizzie was also listed a second time in the directory as Lizzie Serig. Caroline was married, and Walter was still too young (10) to be listed separately.

Matilda's mother, Elizabeth, died on July 24, 1891, at the age of 71. Matilda died ten months later, on May 29, 1892, at the age of 47. I cannot find any information about the cause of her death. Both Matilda and her mother are buried in the Mount Zion Cemetery. The 1892 Wheeling City Directory, the year of her death, shows Matilda Harding still living at 3735 Eoff Street.

Shortly before she died on May 29, 1892, Matilda named her younger brother, August William Serig as the executor of her will and guardian of her minor son, Walter (16). Her will included the following bequests: to her daughter, Elizabeth Moore (wife of John Moore), her sewing machine; to her daughter Caroline Neutzling (wife of Peter Neutzling), fifty dollars and all of her "wearing apparel." The will also stipulated that any real estate was not to be sold until Walter was 21 years old, and upon sale the proceeds were to be divided equally among her four children, and in particular, the proceeds to the daughters were for the daughters and not for their husbands, current or future. The remainder of her estate was to be equally divided between her sons, Louis and Walter.

August William

Matilda's brother, August, had a much more conventional life. He married Mary Virginia Cook (1851 – 1934) on October 26, 1872, when he was 22 years old and she was 20. They had five children between 1873 and 1883, Lillie M. (1873), Harvey W. (1877), George E. (1878), Minnie Bell (1880), and Guy Ford (1883). These five are all members of the second American-born generation of the Augustus line, and are discussed in detail in Chapter VI.

The Augustus line of the Serig family had a lower profile in Wheeling society than the Henry line. However, several property transactions were reported in the local newspapers.

The Wheeling Daily Intelligencer reported on May 29, 1875 that R. H. Cummins and his wife, and R. W. Hazlett and his wife, sold lot No. 20 in square 20, S. W. to August W. Serig, for $900. About nine years later, in August of 1884, August and his wife sold that same lot to Lillie B. Noble for $2,500, and at the same time Lillie B. Noble and her husband sold property in Ohio County to Mary Virginia Serig (August's wife) for $2,200. In March of 1891 August W. Serig and his wife sold lot 14 in square 11 in the Eighth Ward to his sister Matilda Harding.

The only reference I found to involvement in local politics was in August of 1876, when the local newspapers reported that August was a delegate to the county Republican convention from the Ritchie neighborhood. His cousin, Henry J. Serig, was at the Republican convention the next year, so maybe their paths crossed in local party politics.

In 1880, August was living in at 3723 Jacob Street in Wheeling with his wife, Mary, and three of their children. August and Mary owned that house and lived there continuously until sometime between 1911, when the Wheeling City Directory still showed them living on Jacob Street, and 1920, when the federal census showed them living in Los Angeles. Throughout their time in Wheeling, August was described as working as a glass engraver or glass etcher.

In the 1920 census, August, now seventy years old, and his wife, Mary, were living in Los Angeles. They were living with their eldest daughter, Lillie (47), her husband, George Caldabaugh (48), and George's son from a previous marriage, Godfrey (21). August was a glass cutter for a glass company, George was a salesman for a hardware store, and Godfrey was a bookkeeper for a hardware store. August was registered to vote as a Republican.

August William Serig died November 7, 1922 in Los Angeles, just short of his 73rd birthday. In the 1930 census, his widow Virginia (80) was still living in Los Angeles with her daughter and son-in-law, Lillie and George Caldabaugh. George was working as a wholesale hardware stock clerk. Virginia died on October 4, 1934 in Los Angeles at the age of 89. Both August and Virginia are buried in the Inglewood Park Cemetery, in Inglewood, California, a suburb of Los Angeles about five miles northeast of the Los Angeles Airport.

Summary

Augustus (1812 – 1862) and Elizabeth (1820 – 1891) Serig, came from Germany to Wheeling in the 1830s, married and had five children. Although three of these children likely died before reaching adulthood, the other two, Matilda and August William, had nine children between them, all born in Wheeling. Matilda had four children, and August William had five. These nine grandchildren of Augustus Serig are the second American-born generation in the Augustus line, and are discussed in more detail in Chapter VI.

Relation to the Henry Line

No information is available about the extent to which members of the two Serig families interacted socially. However, we can at least examine where they lived in relation to each other.

The two immigrant brothers, Henry J. and Augustus, died in 1851 and 1862, respectively. Shortly after Augustus' death, the main residences for the two families were less than a mile apart. Henry's widow and two sons, Albert (20) and Louis (22), were living at 23rd Street between Main and the river. Augustus' widow and two younger children, Matilda (17) and August William (12), were living at 13th (formerly Chestnut) and Chapline Street (formerly 4th Street), about three-quarters of a mile north.

Over the next decades the two families moved farther apart. By 1890, the two older brothers from the Henry line, Henry J. and Louis, were living close to each other. Henry J. was at 95 Main Street, and Louis was about four blocks away at 218 Kenney (formerly Coal) Street.

Their younger brother, Albert, was farther away. In 1880, he was living in Union Township in Marshall County, south of Wheeling, and in 1900 he was living in Benwood, in Ohio County, but still about five miles south of Wheeling.

The two surviving siblings from the Augustus line, Matilda and August, were also living near each other in South Wheeling. Matilda was at 3735 Eoff Street and August was about two blocks away at 3723 Jacob Street.

About three miles separated Henry and Louis in North Wheeling from Matilda and August in South Wheeling. The two families not only lived in different parts of Wheeling, but they were also buried in different cemeteries, cemeteries that were close to where they lived. The three brothers in the Henry line, their parents and many of their children, were buried in the Mount Wood Cemetery in North Wheeling. Matilda and August and their parents and many of their relatives were buried in the Mount Zion Cemetery, about three miles south in South Wheeling.

Thus, by the end of the first American-born generation of the Serig family it appears they had already divided into the Henry line in North Wheeling and the Augustus line in South Wheeling.

Chapter V
Second Generation – Henry Line

As discussed in Chapter III, Henry E. Serig (1809 – 1851) had three surviving children who together gave him twenty-seven grandchildren. His eldest son, Henry J., had eleven children, his middle son, Louis August, had ten children, and his youngest son, Albert, had six children.

In the family tree below, I have removed Henry E, Serig's two children who did not survive to adulthood, and I have added his twenty-seven grandchildren, the second American-born generation in the Henry line and the subject of this chapter.

As discussed below, only seven of these twenty-seven grandchildren contributed to the third generation of the Henry line in the Wheeling area. The spouses and ancestors for these seven are included in the family tree below. The other twenty either died young (ten), lived to be an adult but never had children (eight), or moved from the Wheeling area (two).

Henry Serig Family Tree

Henry E. Serig (1809 – 1851) m: Mary Christina Dipple (1813 – 1888) before 1836

- Henry J. Serig (1836 – 1916) m: Louisa Maser (1841 – 1928) in 1861
  o Leonora (1862 – 1871)
  o Mary Christina (1865 – 1882)
  o Elizabeth (1867 – 1961)
  o Henry (1870 – 1871)
  o Charles E. (1871 – 1872)
  o Mary (1872 – 1872)
  o Clotilda (1873 – 1968)
  o Laura M. (1876 – 1963) m: Chester Kemple Bell (1874 – 1912) in 1899
  o Lusetta (1879 – 1879)
  o Herman (1881 – 1952)
  o Carl (1884 – 1966)

- Louis August Serig (1843 – 1923) m: Sarah Ann Lewellen (1848 – 1927) in 1868
  o Mary Christina (1869 – 1952)
  o George August (1871 – 1956) m: Maude G. Cotts (1877 – 1923) in 1899
  o Martha Bell (1873 – 1942)
  o Arthur (1874 – ?)
  o Frank (1875 – 1921)
  o Edward (1878 – 1879)
  o Ettie (1880 – 1883)
  o Harry Newton (1883 – 1954) m: Mary K Lynch (1888 – 1947) in 1909
  o Chester L. (1885 – 1970) m: Winnifred Lewellen (1888 – 1945) in 1912
  o Cora (1888 – 1979)

- Arthur Serig (1845 – 1921) m: Sarah Virginia Sykes (1849 – 1944) in 1867
  o William Henry (1868 – 1948) m: Martha Nightengale (1872 – 1952) in 1898
  o Lenora (1870 – 1928)
  o Christina L. (1875 – 1896)
  o Laura (1876 - ?)
  o Sara E. (1878 – 1970) m: August K. Schultze (1877 – 1924) in 1901
  o Albert Garfield (1880 – 1965) m: Anna Schultze (1880 – 1968) in 1906

The Children of
Henry J. Serig (1836 – 1916) and Louisa Maser (1841 – 1928)

Henry J. Serig (1836 – 1916), married Louisa Maser (1841 – 1928) in Wheeling in 1861, and they had eleven children.

Henry and Louisa's children who died young:

- Lenora (1862 – 1871) died just short of her ninth birthday. She is buried in the Mount Wood Cemetery.

- Mary Christina (1865 – 1882) died at the age of 17. She is buried in the Mount Wood Cemetery.

- Henry (1870 – 1871) died three weeks before his first birthday. He is buried in the Mount Wood Cemetery.

- Charles (1871 – 1872) died at the age of about nine months. He is buried in the Mount Wood Cemetery.

- Mary (1872 – 1872) died the same year she was born, perhaps at birth. I cannot find a record of where she is buried.

- Lusetta (1879 – 1879) died at the age of about five weeks. She is buried in the Mount Wood Cemetery.

Henry and Louisa's children who lived to adulthood but had no children:

- Elizabeth (1867 – 1961) died in Wheeling at the age of 93, but she did not marry or have children. She is buried in the Mount Wood Cemetery.

- Clotilda (1873 – 1968) died in Wheeling at the age of 94, but she did not marry or have children. She is buried in the Mount Wood Cemetery.

- Carl (1884 – 1966) married Jessie Mae Lace (1886 – 1948) in 1912, but they had no children. They are both buried in the Greenwood Cemetery in Wheeling.

Henry and Louisa's child who raised his family away from Wheeling:

- Herman (1881 – 1952) moved his family to Indian Springs, Maryland, about 200 miles east of Wheeling before 1930. In the 1930 census he was living there with his wife, Edith (nee Stentzel), and their two sons Charles (19) and Herman (13), and

Edith's mother, Augusta (76). I found no evidence that any of these children returned to the Wheeling area.

Laura was the only child who raised her family in the Wheeling area.

Laura Serig (1876 – 1963) was born on April 5, 1876 in Wheeling. In 1898 she was living with her parents at 95 Main and working as a cashier. She married Chester Kemple Bell (1874 - 1912) in 1899 when she was about twenty-five years old. They had one son, Henry (1902). In 1900, Laura (24) and Chester (25) were living at 438 Market Street in Wheeling. Chester's occupation was "commercial tray (drug)." This may mean that he washed dishes in a drug store. By 1910 they had moved to 212 Railroad Street in Triadelphia, and Chester was working as a commercial traveler. Chester died in 1912, and is buried in the Greenwood Cemetery in Wheeling. At the time of his death Laura was 36 years old, and their son, Henry, was ten. By 1920, Laura had moved back to Wheeling where she was living with her son Henry, and working as an assistant secretary in a paper company. In 1930, Laura was living in Pittsburgh with her son Henry and his wife Kathleen. Henry was working as a draftsman in a factory. By 1940 the family had moved back to Wheeling. Laura was still living with Henry and Kathleen, and Henry was working as a mechanical engineer in a steel factory. Laura died at the age of 87 on July 20, 1963 in Beech Bottom, West Virginia, about 13 miles north of Wheeling, along the Ohio River. She is buried in the Greenwood Cemetery in Wheeling.

The Children of
Louis August Serig (1843 – 1923) and Sarah Lewellen (1848 – 1927)

Louis August Serig (1843 – 1923), married Sarah Ann Lewellen (1848 – 1927) in Wheeling in 1868, and they had ten children.

Louis' children who died young include

- Arthur (1874 - ?) only appears in the 1880 census when he was about six years old, so he likely died young and did not have children. I cannot find where he is buried.

- Edward (1878 – 1879) died at the age of about 14 months. He is buried in the Mount Wood Cemetery.

- Ettie (1880 – 1883) died three months short of her third birthday. She is buried in the Mount Wood Cemetery.

Louis' children who lived to be an adult but did not have children include

- Mary Christina (1869 – 1952) died at the age of 83, but she did not marry or have children. She is buried in the Greenwood Cemetery.

- Frank (1875 – 1921) died in Weston, West Virginia, about 110 miles south of Wheeling, at the age of 44. He did not marry or have children. He is buried in the Mount Wood Cemetery.

- Cora (1888 – 1979) died at the age of 91. She did not marry or have children. She is buried in the Greenwood Cemetery.

Louis' child who moved from the Wheeling area to raise her family is

- Martha (1873 – 1842) married Leo Stender (1881 – 1952) in 1903. They moved to Huntington, West Virginia before 1920, where they were living in 1920 with their son John.

Three children remain who raised families in the Wheeling area: George, Harry, and Chester.

George A. Serig (1871 – 1956) was born on June 21, 1871 in Wheeling. He married Maude G. Cotts (1877 – 1923) in Wheeling in 1899, and they had three sons, Charles Louis (1902), George Irwin (1903), and Hugh (1906). These children are members of the third generation of the Henry line and will be discussed in more detail in Chapter VII. In 1910 George was living at 151 Edgwood Street in Wheeling with his wife, Maude, their three children, his mother-in-law, Charlotte Cotts, and Sadie Church, a school teacher boarder. George worked in a glass business. By 1920, George was the owner of a pottery business. George's wife, Maude, died three years later, in 1923, at the age of 45. George continued living in the house on Edgwood Street for at least the next thirty years, along with several of his children and their growing families. George died in 1956 at the age of 85. George and Maude are both buried in the Greenwood Cemetery.

Harry Newton Serig (1883 – 1954) was born March 17, 1883 in Wheeling. He married Mary K. Lynch (1888 – 1947) in 1909 and they had two children, Harold (1909) and Catherine (1912). These children are members of the third generation of the Henry line and will be discussed in more detail in Chapter VII. In 1910, Harry was living in Wheeling with his wife Mary, and their son Harold. Harry was working as a glass blower. Ten years later Harry and Mary had moved to East First Street in

Wheeling, and Harry was still working as a glass worker. By 1930, the family had moved to Market Street in Wheeling, and Harry was working as a deputy assessor. Mary died in 1947, at the age of 59, and Harry died in 1954, at the age of 71. They are both buried in the Greenwood Cemetery.

Chester Serig (1885 –1970) was born July 27, 1885 in Wheeling. He married Winnifred Lewellen (1888 – 1945) in 1912, and they had one son, Chester Lewellen Serig (1913). Chester, the son, is a member of the third generation of the Henry line and will be discussed in more detail in Chapter VII. In 1920, Chester and Winnifred were living at 711 Zane Street in Martins Ferry, Ohio, and Chester was working as a dyer in a calico mill. By 1930 the family had moved to 806 Indiana Street in Martins Ferry, Ohio, and Chester was working as an assistant shipping clerk in a textile works. They were still at 806 Indiana Street in Martins Ferry, Ohio, ten years later, and Chester was working as a shipping clerk in a dye works. Their son, also Chester, was married and living with them, and working as a crane man in a steel mill. His wife, Margaret, was working as a clerk in a laundry. They also had a lodger living in the house, Ruth Ann Baily, who was working as a teaching nurse in a public school. Winnifred died in 1945 at the age of 57 and is buried in Martins Ferry. Chester died in 1970 in Clearwater Florida at the age of 85, and is buried in Florida.

The Children of
Albert Serig (1845 – 1921) and Sarah Virginia Sykes (1849 – 1944)

Albert (1845 – 1921), married Sarah Virginia Sykes (1849 – 1944) in Wheeling in 1867, and they had six children.

Arthur's child who died young:

- Laura (1876 - ?) likely died as an infant, no known burial.

Arthur's children who lived to adulthood but did not have children:

- Lenora (1870 – 1928) died in Wheeling at the age of 57. She did not marry or have children. She is buried in the Mount Wood Cemetery

- Christina L. (1875 – 1896) died at the age of 20. She did not marry or have children. She is buried in the Mount Wood Cemetery

The three remaining children are William, Sara, and Albert, Jr.

William Henry Serig (1868 – 1948) was born December 29, 1868 in Wheeling. He married Martha N. Nightengale (1872 – 1952) in 1898 and they had two children, Virginia May (1899) and Howard William (1901). The children are members of the third generation of the Henry line and will be discussed in more detail in Chapter VII.

The *Wheeling Daily Intelligencer* reported William and Mattie's wedding on April 29, 1898 as follows:

> At the English Lutheran parsonage in Wheeling last night, Rev. Samuel Schwarm united in marriage Mr. William H. Serig, a popular young millman of Benwood, and Miss Mattie Nighingale, of Park View. The attendants were Mr. August Schultze, of Wheeling, and Miss Sarah Serig, sister of the groom. Following the ceremony, the bridal party was driven to Benwood, where congratulations were showered upon the happy couple.

The bridal party, August Schultze and Sarah Serig, were married three years later in 1901.

In 1900, William and Mattie were living at 4804 Water Street in Benwood, and William was working as a blacksmith.

This item appeared in *The Daily Telegram* on multiple consecutive days in November of 1907:

> "My little girl is subject to colds," says Mrs. Wm. H. Serig, No 41 Fifth St, Wheeling, W. VA. "Last winter she had a severe spell and a terrible cough but I cured her with Chamberlain's Cough Remedy without the aid of a doctor, and my little boy has been prevented many times from having the croup by the timely use of this syrup." This remedy is for sale by all dealers.

By 1910 the family had moved to Triadelphia, and William was still working as a blacksmith. Ten years later, William and Mattie were living at 67 Ohio Street on Wheeling Island with their two children, Howard and Virginia, and Virginia's husband, Carl Neer. William was working as a blacksmith and Carl was working as a printer. Ten years later, the same family members were still living at 67 Ohio Street. At that time, William was working as a custodian in a church and Carl was still working as a printer. The family was still on Ohio Street in 1940. Their son Howard was no longer with them, but Virginia and Carl Neer were still living with them. William was no longer working and Carl was working as a typesetter. William died in 1948 at the age of 79, and Mattie died in 1952 at the age of 80. They are both buried in the Greenwood Cemetery.

Sara Serig (1878 – 1970) was born January 29, 1878 in Wheeling. She married August K. Schultze (1877 – 1924) in 1901 and they had two sons, William (1904) and Clarence (1906). The children are members of the third generation of the Henry line and will be discussed in more detail in Chapter VII. In 1910 Sara and August were living on 33rd Street in Wheeling with their two sons. August was working as a pottery packer. Ten years later they had moved to Eoff Street in Wheeling, and August was a waiter in a restaurant. August died in 1924 in Wheeling at the age of 46, leaving Sara and two nearly grown children, ages 18 and 20. Sara continued living on Eoff Street for at least the next twenty years. In 1930, her younger son, Clarence, was still with her and working in a service station. Her other son, William, was married and living next door with his wife, Emma. In 1940 Sara was still living with Clarence on Eoff Street, and William and Emma and their two daughters were living in the same apartment building. William and Clarence were both gas station attendants. Sara died in 1970 in Saint Clairsville, Ohio, at the age of 92. Both she and her late husband, August, are buried in the Greenwood Cemetery.

Albert Garfield Serig, Jr. (1880 – 1965) was born on July 17, 1880 in Benwood, West Virginia. He married Anna Mary Schultze (1880 – 1968) in 1906. Anna Mary was the sister of Sara Serig's husband, August Schultze. Albert and Anna Mary had two children, Mary Kathleen (1914) and John (1917). The children are members of the third generation of the Henry line and will be discussed in more detail in Chapter VII.

This was reported in the *Wheeling Sunday Register* on July 17, 1887.

> Master Albert Serig entertained a number of his little playmates at his father's residence last evening, the occasion being his eighth birthday [actually his seventh birthday].

In 1910, Albert and Anna Mary were living at 430 South Broadway Street on Wheeling Island, and Albert was a postal carrier. Ten years later they had two children and had moved a short distance to 21½ Ohio Avenue, still on Wheeling Island, and Albert was still working at the post office. By 1930 and continuing to 1940, the family was living at 309 South Penn Street on Wheeling Island, and Albert was still working at the post office. Albert died in 1965 at the age of 84, and Anna died in 1968 at the age of 88. They are both buried in the Greenwood Cemetery.

Summary

Only seven of Henry E. Serig's twenty-seven grandchildren, the second generation in the Henry line, raised their families in the Wheeling area. They are

- Laura M. Serig (1876 – 1963)
- George August Serig (1871 – 1956)
- Harry Newton Serig ((1883 – 1954)
- Chester L. Serig (1885 – 1970)
- William Henry Serig (1868 – 1948)
- Sara E. Serig (1878 – 1970)
- Albert Garfield Serig, Jr. (1880 – 1965)

As discussed in this chapter, those seven had thirteen children, Henry E. Serig's great-grandchildren. Those thirteen are discussed in detail in Chapter VII.

Chapter VI –
Second Generation – Augustus Line

As discussed in Chapter IV, Augustus Serig (1809 – 1851) had two surviving children who together gave him nine grandchildren. Matilda had four children and August William had five children.

As with Henry's family tree in the previous chapter, in Augustus' family tree below, I have removed Augustus' children who did not survive to adulthood, and I have added the nine children of Augustus' two surviving children. These nine children, Augustus Serig's grandchildren, are the second American-born generation in the Augustus line and the subject of this chapter.

As discussed below, only three of these nine grandchildren contributed to the third American-born generation of the Augustus line in the Wheeling area. The spouses and ancestors for these three are included in the family tree below. The other six either died young (one), or lived to be an adult but never had children (five).

Augustus Serig Family Tree

Augustus Serig (1812 – 1862) m: Sophia Mary Elizabeth (1813 – 1888) about 1839.

- Matilda Serig (1845 – 1892) m: Louis Harding (1840 – 1869) in 1867
  - Elizabeth Serig (1864 – 1943) m: John Louis Moore (1863 – 1933) in 1888
  - Caroline Harding (1868 – 1954) m: Peter Nuetzling (1862 – 1927) in 1884
  - Louis August Serig (1871 – 1946) m: Amelia Eberling (1874 – 1923) in 1893
  - Walter Harding (1876 – 1940)

- August William Serig (1849 – 1922) m: Mary Cook (1851 – 1934) about 1873
  - Lillie (1873 – 1954)
  - Harvey (1877 – 1913)
  - George E. (1878 – 1880)
  - Minnie (1880 – 1973)
  - Guy Ford (1883 – 1901)

The Children of Matilda Serig (1845 – 1892)

As explained in Chapter IV, Matilda had only one child during her brief marriage to Louis Harding (1840 - 1869), daughter Caroline Harding, born in 1868. She had another daughter, Elizabeth Serig, born four years earlier in 1864, and two sons born later, Louis Augustus Serig in 1871 and Walter Harding in 1876. The second and fourth children, Caroline and Walter, bore their mother's married last name, Harding, and the first and third childre, Elizabeth and Louis August, bore their mother's maiden name, Serig.

Matilda's youngest child, Walter (1876 – 1940), did not contribute to the next generation. Walter married Elizabeth Herbert (1880 - ?) in 1897. They moved to Pittsburgh sometime before 1930 and did not have any children.

Matilda's remaining three children, Elizabeth, Caroline, and Louis, all married and had children of their own.

Elizabeth "Lizzie" Serig (1864 – 1943) was born on August 7, 1864 in Wheeling. She married John Louis Moore (1863 – 1933) in 1888, and they had two daughters, Henrietta Elizabeth (1889) and Carrie Louise (1891). Carrie was likely named after her aunt, Caroline. These children are part of the third generation of the Augustus line and will be discussed in detail in Chapter VIII. In 1900, Elizabeth and her family were living in Madison, West Virginia, about 200 miles south of Wheeling, next door to her brother Walter Harding. John was working in a feed store. Twenty years later, in 1920, they were living in Pease, Ohio, in Belmont County, across the river and about seven miles north of Wheeling. By this time their daughter Carrie was married to Ralph Woods and they and their three young children were living with her parents. John was a motorman and Ralph was a painter. The whole family was still in Pease in 1930, where both John and Ralph were working as interior decorators. John Moore died in 1933 in Harrison County, Ohio, about 40 miles northwest of Wheeling, at the age of 69. In the 1940 census, Elizabeth, now a widow, was still living in Pease with her daughter Carrie, and son-in-law, Ralph Woods, who was working as a painter. Elizabeth died in 1943 in Belmont County, Ohio, at the age of 79. Both Elizabeth and her late husband, John Moore, are buried in the Greenwood Cemetery in Wheeling.

Caroline Harding (1868 – 1954) was born on February 9, 1868 in Wheeling. She married Peter Neutzling (1862 – 1927) in 1884, and they had seven children, Ella (1884), Elmer (1886), Matilda (1889), Paul (1891), Infant Son (1895), Carrie (1899), and Alma (?). Matilda was likely named after her grandmother, and Carrie shared her name with her cousin who was two years younger. These children are members of the third generation of the Augustus line and will be discussed in detail in Chapter VIII. In 1900, Caroline was living at 208 McMeckin Street in Union, West Virginia, about 260 miles south of Wheeling, with her husband Peter Neutzling and four of their children. Peter was a tube worker, likely making steel tubes in a steel factory. Ten years later Caroline and Peter had returned to Wheeling and were living at 12 Zane Street on Wheeling Island with two of their children, and Peter was still working as a tube worker. Peter died in 1927 in Wheeling, at the age of 65. By 1930 Caroline, now a widow, was living at 14 North Wabash Street on Wheeling Island, with her daughter Carrie, Carrie's husband Frederick Allen, and their children. Caroline died in 1954 in Martins Ferry at the age of 86. Both Caroline and her late husband, Peter Neutzling, are buried in the Mount Zion Cemetery.

Louis August Serig (1871 – 1946) was born on February 17, 1871 in Wheeling. In 1892 Louis was living at 3735 Eoff Street with his mother and worked as a tube worker. He married Amelia Eberling (1874 – 1923) the next year, in 1893, in Moundsville, and they had nine children, Edith (1893), Chester Ellsworth (1895), Vera (1896), Merle (1899), Louis Clifford (1900), Leah (1903), (Helen (1904), Alma (1907), and Elbert (1909). These children are members of the third generation of the Augustus line and will be discussed in more detail in Chapter VIII. In 1901 the family was living at 218 Coal Street (now Kenney Street) in Wheeling, and Louis was the superintendent of the city crematorium. By 1920 the family had moved to 4028 Eoff Street in Wheeling, and Louis was working as a foreman in a tube mill. Louis' wife, Amelia, died in 1923 in Wheeling at the age of 49. Two years later, in 1925, Louis married Jane Francis Hannah (1874 – 1967). Jane had been married previously to Thomas Cook (1860 – 1911), and they had two children, Harold (1898) and Rothbe (1906) Cook. In 1930 Louis and Jane were living at 42 16th Street in Wheeling, and Louis was working as a mechanic in an airplane plant. They were still at 42 16th Street in 1940, and living with them were Louis' stepson, Rothbe Cook, step granddaughter 11-year-old Virginia Cook, and a lodger named William Hayden. Rothbe and William were both salesmen in retail house furnishings. Louis died in 1946 in Wheeling, two weeks short of his 75th birthday. Both Louis and his first wife, Amelia, are buried in the Greenwood Cemetery. Louis' second wife, Jane, died in 1967, at the age of 92, in Westlake, Ohio, a suburb of Cleveland, about 150 miles northwest of Wheeling. She is buried in a cemetery there.

In the 1934 Wheeling City Directory, Louis A. Serig was listed as a pastor in the Reorganized Church of Jesus Christ of the Latter Day Saints (RLDS).[*] I knew that various members of the Serig family were active members of RLDS, but I did not know when or how that connection began. This mention in the 1934 city directory was the earliest indication of that connection that I had found. I asked Karen's uncle, Ward Serig (see Chapter XIV), if he knew how and when the family first became involved with RLDS, and this is what he told me.

> Louis A. Serig was riding home from work on a trolley car with a friend. This was before he was married. His friend asked him which church he belonged to and Louis told him that he was Lutheran. His friend then asked, "Why don't you join a church named after Jesus Christ?" Louis replied that maybe he would and started going to the RLDS church with his friend and eventually joined. As far as I know he was the first Serig to become a member of the church.

Apparently, when Louis later married, he married into a family that was also RLDS. Ward also told me this story.

> The woman he [Louis] married has an interesting story which a friend wrote me about several years ago. Louis' wife was Amelia Eberling. . . The Eberling family were long time RLDS. My friend wrote me that Amelia's brother, Frank, was married to a lady named Josephine, who was a granddaughter of Alexander Hale Smith, the first Presiding Patriarch of the RLDS Church, and the son of Joseph Smith, Jr., the founder of the LDS church. Frank and Josephine had two daughters. Interestingly one was a classmate of mine at Graceland College and the other was a classmate of Joe's. At that time, we didn't know the family connection, but it turns out they were Dad's first cousins.

---

[*] The Reorganized Church of Jesus Christ of Latter Day Saints broke away from the Church of Jesus Christ of Latter Day Saints in 1860, and was renamed as the Community of Christ in 2001.

The Children of
August William Serig (1845 – 1892) and Mary Cook (1851 – 1934)

Matilda's younger brother, August William Serig, married Mary Virginia Cook in Wheeling in 1873. They had the following five children, none of whom had children of their own.

- Lillie (1873 – 1954) married Joseph Dudley in 1896, when she was 23 years old. After divorcing Joseph, she married George Caldabaugh in 1910. By 1920 Lillie and George had moved to Los Angeles. It does not appear that Lillie had children with either husband.

- Harvey (1877 – 1913) moved to Los Angeles with his parents in 1911 or 1912. Harvey died there in 1913 at the age of 36. He never married or had children.

- George (1878 – 1880) died in Wheeling at the age of twenty-and-a-half months. He is buried in the Mount Zion Cemetery.

- Minnie (1880 – 1973) married Frederick Bell in 1901 in Wheeling. They moved to Los Angeles before 1910. They did not have any children.

- Guy (1883 – 1901) died in Wheeling in 1901 at the age of 18. He did not marry or have children. He is buried in the Mount Zion Cemetery.

Summary

Only three of Augustus Serig's grandchildren, the second generation in the Augustus line, raised their families in the Wheeling area. Those three are

- Elizabeth Serig (1864 – 1943)
- Caroline Harding ((1868 – 1954)
- Louis August Serig (1871 – 1946)

As discussed in this chapter, those three had eighteen children, Augustus Serig's great-grandchildren. Those eighteen are discussed in detail in Chapter VIII.

Relation to the Henry Line

This chapter discussed three individuals from the second generation of the Augustus line who remained in Wheeling. The previous chapter discussed their seven second cousins from the Henry line who remained in Wheeling. These ten were born between 1868 and 1885. This section describes where in the Wheeling area these families lived in relation to each other. I focus primarily on 1910, when these descendants were of the age to get married and have children.

As described in Chapter IV, the first cousin descendants of the immigrant brothers, the first generation of the Serig family in Wheeling, had eventually settled in different parts of Wheeling. Henry J. and Louis from the Henry line were living about three miles north of Matilda and August from the Augustus line. The two lines were also buried in different cemeteries, close to their homes. However, their children, the second generation of the two lines, were more scattered around the Wheeling area.

The seven second generation descendants of Henry E. Serig who remained in the Wheeling area were children of three of his sons, Henry J. Serig, Louis August Serig, and Albert Serig.

In 1910, Henry J.'s daughter, Laura, and her husband Chester Bell, were living in Triadelphia, east of Wheeling.

In 1910, Louis August's oldest son, George, was living at 151 Edgwood Street, about 3.5 miles east of downtown Wheeling. His middle son, Harry, was married and living in an alley off Main Street in North Wheeling. His youngest son, Chester, was still living with his parents on Kenney (formerly Coal) Street.

In 1910, Albert's oldest son, William, was living in Triadelphia, east of Wheeling, near his cousin Laura. His daughter, Sara, and her husband, August Schultze, and living at 47 33rd Street in South Wheeling. Another son, Albert Jr., was married and living at 430 South Broadway on Wheeling Island.

The three second generation descendants of Augustus Serig who remained in the Wheeling area were all children of his daughter, Matilda, Elizabeth, Caroline, and Louis August.

In 1910, Elizabeth and her husband John Moore were living at 1039 Main Street in Wheeling. Caroline and her husband Peter Neutzling were living at 12 Zane Street on Wheeling Island. Louis August was living at 4028 Eoff Street in South Wheeling.

Taken together, by 1910 the second American-born generation was fairly scattered around the Wheeling area, and for the most part, members of the Henry and Augustus lines were not in close proximity to each other. One exception was that Albert from the Henry line and his second cousin, Caroline from the Augustus line, were both living on Wheeling Island, about a half mile apart. Although Caroline was twelve years older than Albert, their Serig parents, who were first cousins, were the same age, suggesting they may have interacted as children if not as adults. This in turn suggests that Caroline and Albert may have at least been aware of the family connection even if they did not interact as adults.

Chapter VII
Third Generation – Henry Line

As discussed in Chapter V, Henry E. Serig (1809 – 1851) had seven grandchildren who remained the Wheeling area and who together gave him thirteen great-grandchildren.

In the family tree below, I have removed Henry E. Serig's twenty grandchildren who did not raise families in the Wheeling area, and I have added his thirteen great-grandchildren, the third American-born generation in the Henry line and the subject of this chapter.

As discussed below, only six of these thirteen great-grandchildren contributed to the fourth generation of the Henry line in the Wheeling area. The spouses and ancestors for these six are included in the family tree below. The other seven either lived to be an adult but never had children (three), or moved from the Wheeling area (four).

The Children of
Laura Serig (1876 – 1963) and Chester Bell (1874 – 1912)

Henry Bell (1902 – 1975) was born on November 11, 1902 in Wheeling. Henry married Katherine Flanagan (1903 – 1983) in 1927, and they had two daughters, Jean (1928) and Eleanor (1935). The children are members of the fourth generation of the Henry line and will be discussed in more detail in Chapter IX. Henry's father had died in 1912, when Henry was ten years old. After his father's death, Henry and his mother returned to Wheeling before moving to Pittsburgh and then back to Wheeling. By 1940, the family had moved to 103 Maple Avenue. Henry had completed one year of college, and he was working as a mechanical engineer. Henry died in Wheeling in 1975. I cannot find where he is buried. His widow, Kathleen, died in Staunton, Virginia in 1983, apparently after following one of her daughters there.

Henry E. Serig Family Tree

Henry E. Serig (1809 – 1851) m: Mary Christina Dipple (1813 – 1888)

- Henry J. Serig (1836 – 1916) married Louisa Maser (1841 – 1928) in 1861
  - Laura Serig (1876 – 1963) married Chester Bell (1874 – 1912) in 1899
    - Henry Bell (1902 – 1975) m: Katherine Flanagan (1903 – 1983) in 1927
- Louis August Serig (1843 – 1923) married Sarah Lewellen (1848 – 1927) in 1868
  - George August Serig (1871 – 1956) married Maud Cotts (1877 – 1923) in 1899
    - Charles Louis Serig (1901 – 1981) m: Wilma King (1900 – 1983) in 1922
    - George Serig (1903 – 1984)
    - Hugh Serig (1905 – 1984)
  - Harry Newton Serig (1883 – 1954) married Mary Lynch (1888 – 1947) in 1909
    - Harold Serig (1909 – 1954) m: Gertrude Foran (1909 – 1982) in 1935
    - Anna Catherine Serig (1911 – 1985) m: John McMullen (1897 – 1968) in 1938
  - Chester L. Serig (1885 – 1970) m: Winifred Lewellyn (1888 – 1945) in 1912
    - Chester L. Serig Jr. (1913 – 2004)
- Arthur Serig (1845 – 1921) m: Sarah Virginia Sykes (1849 – 1944) in 1867
  - William H. Serig (1868 – 1948) m: Martha Nightengale (1972 – 1952) in 1898
    - Virginia Serig (1899 – 1991)
    - Howard Serig (1901 – 1989)
  - Sara Serig (1878 – 1970) m: August Schultze (1877 – 1924) in 1901
    - William Schultze (1903 – 1979) m: Emma King (1908 – 1994) in 1925
    - Clarence Schultze (1906 – 1985)
  - Albert Jr. Serig (1880 – 1965) m: Anna Mary Schultze (1880 – 1968) in 1906
    - Mary Kathleen Serig (1914 – 2009) m: Robert Muldoon (1916 – 1996) in 19??
    - John Serig (1917 – 2004)

The Children of
George August Serig (1871 – 1956) and Maud Cotts (1871 – 1923)

Charles Louis Serig (1901 – 1981) was born on January 21, 1901 in Wheeling. He married Wilma King (1900 – 1983) in 1922, and they had one son, James Louis Serig (1929). James is a member of the fourth generation of the Henry line and will be discussed in more detail in Chapter IX. In 1930, Charles was living at 151 Edgwood Street, about three-and-a-half miles east of downtown Wheeling, with his wife, their son, his father, George, his brother, George Jr., and his aunt, Cora. Charles' mother, Maude, had died in 1923. Charles was a service manager at an auto dealership and his father was a foreman at a pottery factory. Ten years later, the family was still living on Edgwood Street, and Charles was a laborer in the tobacco industry and his father was a salesman of "retail extracts." When Charles registered for the draft in 1941, he was still living on Edgwood Street and working at Bloch Brothers Tobacco Co. Charles died on June 11, 1981, at the age of 80. He is buried in the Greenwood Cemetery in Wheeling alongside his wife, Wilma, and near the graves of his parents. The markers on those graves, George and Wilma's, and the marker for George's parents, were the grave markers that Amy had asked her aunt Karen about.

George Irvin Serig (1903 – 1984) was born on June 13, 1903 in Wheeling. He married Sarah Reass (1911 – 1999) in 1934 in Jackson, West Virginia, about 130 miles south of Wheeling. George and Sarah had three children, Sonya (1938), Dennis (1943) and George Michael (1947). In 1940 they were living at 800 North Market Street in Wheeling with their young daughter, Sonya, Sarah's father, George, and her brother, George Jr. George Serig was working as a collector for the City of Wheeling. George Reass Sr. was retired and George Reass Jr. was working at a gas station. George Serig died in Newport News, Virginia in 1984, and Sarah also died in Newport News, in 1999. They are both buried there. It appears that they moved from Wheeling while the children were still relatively young. Sonya went to high school in Hampton, Virginia, and both Dennis and George Michael went to high school in Newport News, Virginia. None of the children returned to Wheeling to live.

Hugh Serig (1905 – 1984) was born on June 30, 1905 in Wheeling. He married Elizabeth Pennington in 1929, and they had one child, Robert (1940). In 1940 they were living in Washington, Pennsylvania where Hugh worked as the manager of a retail dairy business. He was still living in Washington, Pennsylvania at the time of his death in 1984, and Elizabeth was still in Washington at the time of her death in 2003. I cannot find where they are buried. Their son, Robert, died in 2012 in South Carolina.

The Children of
Harry Serig (1883 – 1954) and Mary Lynch (1888 – 1947)

Harold Thomas Serig (1909 – 1952) was born on August 29, 1909 in Wheeling. He married Gertrude Foran (1909 – 1982) in 1935 and they had two children, Patricia Catherine (1936) and Mary Ann (1940). The children are members of the fourth generation of the Henry line and will be discussed in more detail in Chapter IX. When Harold registered for the draft in 1940 the family was living at 629 Market Street in Wheeling, and Harold was working for Wheeling News Publishing. Harold died in 1952 at the age of 43. Gertrude remarried in 1959, to James Alvin Bartollas (1900 – 2000). James' first wife, Anna Helena Maloney (1902 – 1952), had also died in 1952 at the age of 49. Gertrude died in 1982 at the age of 72, and James died in 2000 at the age of 100. All four, Harold, Gertrude, James and Anna, are buried in the Mount Calvary Cemetery in Wheeling.

Anna Catherine Serig (1911 – 1985) was born on May 25, 1911. She married John McMullen (1897 – 1968) in 1938, and they had three children, Joseph (1940), Mary Emily (1945), and Sally (?). The children are members of the fourth generation of the Henry line and will be discussed in more detail in Chapter IX. In 1940, Anna and John were living with Anna's parents at 629 Market Street in Wheeling. John was a foreman for a construction company and his father-in-law was a watchman at a dry goods store. His draft registration card for World War II curiously shows his place of residence as 404 Maple Place in Martins Ferry, but his mailing address as 629 Market Street in Wheeling, and he reported as his contact for someone who will always know where he is, Miss Myrtle McMullen at 404 Maple Street in Martins Ferry. Myrtle is John's older sister. John died in 1968 at the age of 70, and Anna died in 1985 at the age of 74. They are both buried in the Greenwood Cemetery.

The Children of
Chester Serig (1885 – 1970) and Winifred Lewellen (1888 – 1945)

Chester L. Serig Jr. (1913 – 2004) was born on July 14, 1913 in Martins Ferry. He married Margaret Williamson (1916 – 1985) in 1939, and they had one child, James F. (1943). Margaret died in Florida in 1985. Her obituary said that she had gone to Florida in 1963, and that she was survived by her husband Chester L. and her son, James F. both living in

Florida. Chester married Dorothy Wilma (Kauffman) Byrd in 1990. Chester died in Florida in 2004. An internet search indicates that Chester's son, James, is still living in Florida.

The Children of
William Serig (1868 – 1988) and Martha Nightengale (1872 – 1952)

Virginia May Serig (1899 – 1991) was born on March 16, 1899 in Wheeling. She married Carl Neer (1895 – 1964) in 1916 in Wheeling. They did not have any children. Carl died in 1964 at the age of 68, and Virginia died in 1991 at the age of 91. They are both buried in the Greenwood Cemetery.

Howard William Serig (1901 – 1989) was born on July 13, 1901 in Benwood. He married Vivian Christine Fiveash (1912 – 1975) in New York in 1939. At the time she was a nurse in the Army and he was a West Point graduate and an Army Captain. They had one son, Howard William Jr. (1942). According to the 1940 census, Howard Sr. was living at Fort Monmouth in New Jersey. Vivian died in New Jersey in 1975 at the age of 63. At the time of her death, their son, Howard, was living in Falls Church, Virginia. Howard Sr. died in 1989 at the age of 87. Both Howard Sr. and Vivian are buried in the Greenwood Cemetery in Wheeling. Other than to bury his parents, it appears that Howard Jr. did not return to Wheeling to live. He married Robin Eleanor Grubmeyer in 1973 in Vermont. A 2007 publication of the Stern Business School at New York University reported that Howard W. Serig, Jr. (BS '64, MBA '67), of Vienna, Virginia, had retired from the US Department of Transportation, where he served as a policy analyst. An internet search indicates that Howard Jr. and Robin still live in Vienna, Virginia.

The Children of
Sara Serig (1878 – 1970) and August Schultze (1877 – 1924)

William John Albert Schultze (1903 – 1979) was born on August 16, 1903 in Wheeling. He married Emma King (1908 – 1994) in 1925 in Brooke County, West Virginia, just north of Wheeling. They had two daughters, Dorothy (1925) and Ilene May (1931). The children are members of the fourth generation of the Henry line and will be discussed in more detail in Chapter IX. In the 1940 census all four members of the family were living together in Wheeling at 3318 Eoff Street. William was an attendant at a gas station. William died in 1979 at the age of 75, and Emma died in 1994 at the age of 85. I cannot find information about where they are buried.

Clarence R. Schultze (1906 – 1985) was born on February 22, 1906 in Wheeling. He married Madeline Wagner (1911 – 1947) in 1941. After Madeline's death in 1947, at the age of 36, Clarence married Sophia Watkins (nee Otvenoski) in 1951. Sophia had previously been married to Elwood Watkins. Clarence did not have children with either wife. Clarence died in 1985 at the age of 79. Clarence and Madeline are both buried in the Greenwood Cemetery.

The Children of
Albert Serig (1880 – 1965) and Anna Mary Schultze (1880 – 1968)

Mary Kathleen Serig (1914 – 2009) was born on August 16, 1914 in Wheeling. She married Robert Muldoon (1916 – 1996), and they had two children, Sally (1950) and Robert (1957). The children are members of the fourth generation in the Henry line, and are described further in Chapter IX. In 1940, Mary Kathleen was living at 309 South Penn Street with her parents and younger brother, Jack. Robert Muldoon Sr. died in 1996 at the age of 80, and Mary Kathleen died in 2009 at the age of 95. Both are buried in the Greenwood Cemetery.

John W. Serig (1917 – 2004) was born on February 1, 1917 in Wheeling. He married Mary Yeager (1924 – 1975), year unknown. Mary died in 1975 at the age of 51. After Mary's death, John married Rose Lee Crago (nee Goosman, 1919 – 2018) who had previously been married to Lee Roy Crago. John died in 2004 at the age of 87. John and Mary are both buried in the Greenwood Cemetery. It does not appear that John had children by either spouse. Further information about John is provided in Chapter XV.

Summary

Only six of Henry E. Serig's great-grandchildren, the third American-born generation in the Henry line, raised their families in the Wheeling area. Those six are

- Henry Bell (1902 – 1975)
- Charles Louis Serig (1901 – 1981)
- Harold Thomas Serig (1909 – 1952)

- Anna Catherine Serig (1911 – 1985)
- William Schultze (1903 – 1979)
- Mary Kathleen Serig (1914 – 2009)

As discussed in this chapter, those six had twelve children, Henry E. Serig's 2x great-grandchildren. Those twelve are discussed in detail in Chapter IX.

Chapter VIII
Third Generation – Augustus Line

As discussed in Chapter VI, Augustus Serig (1809 – 1851) had three grandchildren who raised their families in the Wheeling area. These three grandchildren gave him eighteen great-grandchildren

As previously, I have removed from the family tree below Augustus' six grandchildren who did not raise children in the Wheeling area, and I have added his eighteen great-grandchildren, the third American-born generation in the Augustus line and the subject of this chapter.

As discussed below, only seven of these eighteen great-grandchildren contributed to the fourth generation of the Henry line in the Wheeling area. The spouses and ancestors for these seven are included in the family tree below. The other eleven either died young (three), lived to be an adult but never had children (three), or moved away from the Wheeling area (five).

The Children of
Elizabeth Serig (1864 – 1943) and John Moore (1863 – 1933)

Henrietta Elizabeth Moore (1889 – 1982) was born on September 12, 1889 in Wheeling. She married Louis O'Hare (1879 – 1948) in 1905, and they had at least six children, Louise (1906), Charles (1907), Elizabeth (1910), Louis (1912), Thomas (1914), and John (1916). In 1910 Henrietta and Louis were living in Wheeling with three young children. Ten years later they were living in Cleveland with six children, but by 1930 they had moved to Baltimore. Louis died in 1948 in Baltimore, at the age of 68. Henrietta died in 1982 in Maryland at the age of 92. They are both buried in Baltimore, and none of the children returned to the Wheeling area.

Carrie Louise Moore (1891 – 1981) was born December 23, 1891 in Wheeling, and is likely named after her aunt, Caroline. She married Ralph Woods (1890 – 1955) in 1912, and they had three children, Henrietta (1913), Ralph (1916) and Marjorie (1919), who are all fourth-generation descendants of Augustus, and are discussed further in Chapter X. In 1920, Carrie and Ralph were living with their three children and Carrie's parents in Pease Township, Ohio, across the river and about seven miles north of

Wheeling. Ralph was working as a painting contractor. Ten years later they were still in Pease, still with Ralph's parents, and Ralph's work was listed as an interior decorator. In 1940 they were still in Pease. Ralph's mother was still with them, but his father had died. Ralph's occupation was once again listed as a painting contractor. Ralph Woods Sr. died in 1955 in Martins Ferry, Ohio, at the age of 64. Carrie died in 1981 at the age of 89 in Arlington, TX, where her son, Ralph Jr., was living. Both Carrie and Ralph are buried in the Greenwood Cemetery in Wheeling.

Augustus Serig Family Tree

Augustus Serig (1812 – 1862) m: Sophia Mary Elizabeth (1813 – 1888) about 1839.

- Matilda Serig (1845 – 1892) m: Louis Harding (1840 – 1869)
  - Elizabeth Serig (1864 – 1943) m: John Louis Moore (1863 – 1933) in 1888
    - Henrietta Moore (1889 – 1982)
    - Carrie L. Moore (1891 – 1981) m: Ralph Woods (1890 – 1955) in 1912
  - Caroline Harding (1868 – 1954) m: Peter Nuetzling (1862 – 1927) in 1884
    - Ella Clara Neutzling (1884 – 1886)
    - Elmer H. Neutzling (1888 – 1956) m: Myrtle Williams (1886 – 1974) in 1907
    - Matilda Neutzling (1889 – 1940) m: Gomer Liston (1888 – 1964) in 1908
    - Paul Neutzling (1891 – 1977)
    - Infant Son Neutzling (1895 – 1895)
    - Alma Neutzling (? – 1898)
    - Carrie Neutzling (1899 – 1980) m: Fred Allen (1888 - 1974) in 1916.
  - Louis August Serig (1871 – 1946) m: Amelia Eberling (1874 – 1923) in 1893
    - Edith May Serig (1893 – ?)
    - Chester E. Serig (1895 – 1958)
    - Vera Serig (1896 – 1976)
    - Merle Virginia Serig (1898 – 1923)
    - Louis Clifford Serig (1900 – 1977) m: Loma Ward (1901 – 1938) in 1921
    - Leah A. Serig (1902 – 1995) m: George Ries (1896 – 1974) in 1921
    - Helen M. Serig (1904 – 1988) m: Charles H. Dueker (1899 – 1965) in 1922
    - Alma F. Serig (1906 – 1978)
    - Elbert R. Serig (1908 – 1974)

The Children of
Caroline Harding (1868 – 1954) and Peter Neutzling (1862 - 1927)

Ella Neutzling (1884 – 1886) died at about the age of eighteen months. She is buried in the Mount Zion Cemetery.

Elmer Neutzling (1886 – 1956) was born on September 19, 1886 in Wheeling, He married Myrtle Williams (1886 – 1974) in Ohio County, West Virginia, in 1907, and they had six children, Madolyn Dorothy (1909), Leona V. (1910), Janice Ellen (1913), Eleanor M. (1914), Elmer S. (1919), and Rosalie C. (1921). These six children are part of the fourth American-born generation of the Augustus line and are discussed further in Chapter X. Prior to their marriage, on February 20, 1906, Elmer and Myrtle starred in a local production of a play at the Carroll Club Auditorium, "A Confederate Spy," described as "A beautiful story of the late Civil War." Admission was 25 cents, 10 cents extra for a reserved seat. In 1910, Elmer and Myrtle were living at 409 North Wabash Street on Wheeling Island with their first child, and Elmer was working as a newspaper pressman. Ten years later, they had moved to 73 Indiana Street on Wheeling Island with five of their eventual six children, and a boarder, 52-year-old Usauld Kreenter. Elmer was still working as a pressman. In 1930, Elmer and Myrtle were living at 118 North Wabash Street on Wheeling Island with five of their children. In 1940 Elmer and Myrtle were living at 2745 Wood Street in South Wheeling with their youngest child. Elmer died in 1956 in Canton, Ohio at the age of 69, and he is buried in the Forest Hill Cemetery in Canton. Myrtle died in Leavittsburg, Ohio, about 100 miles north of Wheeling, in 1974 at the age of 88.

Matilda Neutzling (1889 – 1940) was born in April 1889, in Wheeling, and was apparently named after her maternal grandmother, Matilda, who was still living at the time of Matilda's birth. Matilda married Gomer Thomas Liston (1888 – 1964) in 1908, and they had two sons, Gomer (1911) and Vernon (1912), who are fourth generation descendants of Augustus and are discussed further in Chapter X. In 1920, Matilda and Gomer were living near her cousin, Carrie, in Pease Township, Ohio, across the river from Wheeling. Gomer was working as an electrician. In 1930 and 1940, the family was still living in Pease Township, and Gomer was working as a railroad inspector. Matilda died in 1940 in Painesville, Ohio, just northeast of Cleveland, at the age of 51. Her death certificate indicates she was buried in Bridgeport, Ohio. Gomer married Margaret Bell (1897 – 1969) in Ohio County, West Virginia in 1943. Gomer died in 1964, and Margaret died in 1969. Gomer and Margaret are both buried in the Greenwood Cemetery in Wheeling.

Paul Louis Neutzling (1891 – 1977) was born August 1891 in West Virginia, and married Irene Kurner (1888 – 1983) in 1916. From 1920 through 1940 they lived at 10 Mount Wood Road in Wheeling. Irene's brother, William Kurner lived with them throughout that time. In 1920, Paul was a pressman for a newspaper, and in 1930 he was an agent for the "State Compenster." In 1940, he was a safety engineer for a coal mining company. Paul died in 1977 at the age of 85, and Irene died in 1983 at the age of 95. I cannot find where they are buried. It appears they had no children.

Infant Son Neutzling (1895 – 1895) was premature and died the day after his birth. He is buried in the Mount Zion Cemetery.

Carrie Neutzling (1899 – 1980) was born August 15, 1899 in West Virginia, and was apparently named after her mother. She married Fred Allen (1888 – 1974) in 1916. They had four children, Guy (1917), Matilda (1918), Carl (1926) and Glen (1929). These children are all fourth-generation descendants of Augustus, and are discussed further in Chapter X. Fred served in World War I in Battery E of the 104th Field Artillery, 27th Division, and returned from France aboard the U.S.S. America in March 1919. In 1920, Carrie and Fred lived at 317 West Wabash Street on Wheeling Island. Fred was a street car conductor for Traction Company. By 1930 the family had moved to 14 North Wabash Street on Wheeling Island. Carrie and Fred now had four children and Carrie's mother was living with them. Fred was still working as a street car conductor. Fred Allen died in 1974 at the age of 86, and Carrie died in 1980, at the age of 80. I cannot find where they are buried.

Alma Neutzling (1988 – 1988) died as an infant, and is buried in the Mount Zion Cemetery.

The Children of
Louis A. Serig (1871 – 1946) and Amelia Eberling (1874 – 1923)

Edith May Serig (1893 – ?) was born about 1893 in Wheeling. She married Paul H. Braman (1891 – 1954) in 1912, and they had four children, Dorothy (1913), Arthur (1915), Robert (1923), and William (1929). In 1920 the family was living with Paul's brother in Akron, Ohio, and in 1930 and 1940 they were living in Erie, New York. Paul died in 1954 in Blasdell, New York, eight miles south of Buffalo. I cannot find information on Edith's death. None of the children returned to the Wheeling area.

Chester Ellsworth Serig (1895 – 1958) was born April 13, 1895 in Wheeling. He married Elsie Wilson (1902 – 1976) in 1917, and they had three children, Chester (1925), Wesley (1927), and Gail (1930). In 1930, Chester and Elsie were living in Harvey, Illinois, about 22 miles south of Chicago, and Chester was working as a toolmaker in a paint factory. By 1940 they had moved to Chicago. Chester died in Chicago in 1958, and Elsie died in Madison, Wisconsin in 1976. None of the children returned to the Wheeling area.

Vera Serig (1896 – 1976) was born October 26, 1896 in Wheeling. She married John D. Carlisle (1889 – 1965) in 1914 and they had three children, James W. (1918), Glenn Richard (1923), and Lois A. (1932). In 1920, Vera and John lived in Goshen, Ohio, about 30 miles northwest of Cincinnati, where John worked as a coal miner. They stayed in Goshen through at least 1940, and John worked variously as a Ford car salesman and a tractor salesman. John died in 1965 and Vera died in 1976 and both are buried in New Philadelphia, Ohio, about sixty miles northwest of Wheeling, as are all three of their children.

Merle Serig (1899 – 1923) was born on August 16, 1898 in Wheeling. She married Roy Baker (1896 – 1967) in 1920. Merle died February 18, 1923 in Wheeling, at the age of 24. She is buried in the Greenwood Cemetery in Wheeling. It appears that Merle and Roy did not have any children.

Louis Clifford Serig (1900 – 1977) was born July 16, 1900 in Wheeling. He married Loma Ward (1901 – 1938) on January 21, 1921. In 1920, Loma was living at 120 South Huron Street, on Wheeling Island, with her parents and ten brothers and sisters. She had another brother who had died in infancy, and two more siblings were yet to be born. Louis' parents and five of his eight siblings were living at 4028 Eoff Street, on the mainland about three miles from the Ward family. Louis' father, was a foreman in a tube mill.

In 1920, Louis was serving in the Marine Corps, where he was variously stationed in Philadelphia, Parris Island, South Carolina, and Quantico, Virginia. At the time of their wedding, in January 1921, Louis was stationed in Philadelphia, and this notice appeared in *The Wheeling Intelligencer* on January 27, 1921.

> The marriage of Miss Leona Ward, daughter of Mr. and Mrs. Chester A. Ward, to Sergeant Louis C. Serig, son of Mr. and Mrs. Louis Serig, Sr., of South Eoff Street, which was solemnized Monday evening at the parsonage of the Zane Street M. E. church, came as a surprise to the many friends of the couple who are extending their best wishes.
>
> The groom is serving in the U.S. Marine Corps. The bride is widely known.

The newspaper gave Loma's name incorrectly as Leona and gave her father's name, Charles, incorrectly as Chester. No explanation was given for why the marriage was a surprise. Ten months later, on November 26, 1921, the following appeared in *The Wheeling Intelligencer*:

> Sergeant and Mrs. Louis Serig will leave this evening for Quantico, VA., where Sergt. Serig will join his company in the U.S. marine corps at their winter quarters.
>
> While in the city, Mr. and Mrs. Serig were the guests of Mr. and Mrs. Louis A. Serig of the South Side and Mr. and Mrs. Charles A. Ward of the Island. They arrived here last Sunday from Cleveland where Sergt. Serig has been stationed since last July.

Louis and Loma had five sons, Louis Albert (1922 – 1923), Charles (1923), Jack (1928), Ward (1933), and Joe (1936), who are all fourth-generation descendants of Augustus. Charles and his descendants are discussed in Chapter XIII. His three younger brothers and their descendants are discussed in Chapter XIV.

In 1930, Louis and his family were living at 270 Wood Street in Wheeling and he was working as a bookkeeper. In 1934, the family lived at 2717 Jacob Street in Wheeling. Loma died in 1938 at the age of 36 and is buried in the Greenwood Cemetery.

In 1939, Louis married Mary Alice Coulter (1904 – 1968) in Wheeling. The next year, in 1940, Louis, Mary Alice, and the four boys were living in Portsmouth, Virginia. Louis divorced Mary Alice in Brevard, Florida in 1944, and then married Dorothy Virginia Whitecotton (1913 – 1984), originally of Wheeling, in 1946. They must have divorced because Dorothy later married Charles Head in Oklahoma in 1967 and they settled in Granbury, Texas, where she died in 1984.

Louis spent twenty years as a civil service administrator at the Guantanamo Naval Base in Cuba from 1945 to 1965. He was a member of the Loyal Order of Moose, and sent his younger sons to Mooseheart Child City and School, about 38 miles west of Chicago, when he took employment at Guantanamo.

Sometime after his divorce from Dorothy Whitecotten, Louis married Elizabeth Cecilia Monaghan (1904 – 1986). I can't find when they married, but a document shows her traveling to Miami from her permanent address at Guantanamo in Cuba in 1962 as Elizabeth Serig. Elizabeth was born in Scotland and came to the United States as a baby in 1904. The family settled in Southampton, Virginia. She married Thomas Charles Kinney in 1923 in Camden, North Carolina, and they divorced in 1930 in Norfolk, Virginia. They had one daughter, Margaret Elizabeth Kinney (1924 – 1993).

Louis died on February 25, 1977 in Miami, Florida at the age of 76. He is buried in Ocala, Florida. Elizabeth died on February 13, 1986 in Ocala, Florida. I cannot find where she is buried.

Leah Serig (1902 – 1995) was born July 25, 1902 in Wheeling. She married George Ries (1896 – 1974) in 1921, and they had three children, George Harold (1925), Glenn Robert (1928), and Kathryn June (1934). These children are all fourth generation American-born descendants of Augustus, and are discussed in detail in Chapter X. In 1930 and 1940 they were living at 2627 Jacob Street in Wheeling, near Leah's brother, Louis, and George Sr. was a bookkeeper/accountant for a steel company. George died in 1974 at the age of 77, and Leah died in 1995 at the age of 93. I can't find information on where either of them is buried.

Helen Marguerite Serig (1904 – 1988) was born November 27, 1904 in Wheeling. She married Charles H. Dueker (1899 – 1965) in 1922, and they had three children, Lois I. (1926), Elizabeth (1928), and Richard (1940).

The children are all fourth generation American-born descendants of Augustus, and are discussed in detail in Chapter X. In 1930 they were living at 103 N. 10th Street in Wheeling, and Charles was working in a plumbing and heating shop. In 1940 they were living at 2518 Chapline Street in Wheeling, and Charles had his own plumbing business. Helen died in 1988 in Wheeling at the age of 83. I can't find where she is buried.

Alma Serig (1906 – 1978) was born November 27, 1906 in Wheeling. In 1924 she was living at 4028 Eoff Street, next door to her parents, and working as a phone operator. In 1930 she boarded with Edna Thomas and Edna's eight-year-old son Russell, at 112 Chillicothe Road in Kirtland, Ohio, about 23 miles northeast of Cleveland, and worked as a telephone operator. Alma married George W. Thomas (1895 – 1967) in 1934 in Ohio County, West Virginia. They did not have any children. In 1935 they were living in Independence Missouri, but by 1940 they had returned to Wheeling. Alma died February 21, 1978 in Martins Ferry, at the age of 71. I cannot find where she is buried.

Elbert Serig (1908 – 1974) was born October 25, 1908 in Wheeling. He married Helen Lulkowski (1909 – 1985) in Lake, Indiana in 1928. They had two daughters, Norlene (1929) and Shirley (1934), and one son, Dale (1948). From at least 1930 they lived in the Chicago area, and did not return to live in Wheeling. Elbert died in 1974 at the age of 65, and Helen died in 1985 at the age of 74, both near Chicago.

Chapter VI described how Louis A. Serig, Elbert's father, became a member of the Reorganized Church of Jesus Christ of the Latter Day Saints (RLDS). Some his children and grandchildren were also actively involved in the church. This is what Ward Serig (see Chapter XIV) told me about that involvement.

> The other family members who I recall as being ministers in the church were Vera's son Glenn, and perhaps his older brother, James. Helen's husband, Charles was an elder. The youngest son, Elbert, was also an elder. Elbert's son, Dale, who lives near Chicago is also an elder.

Summary

Seven of Augustus Serig's great-grandchildren, the third American-born generation in the Augustus line, raised their families in the Wheeling area. Those seven are

- Carrie Louis Moore (1891 – 1981)
- Elmer Neutzling (1886 – 1956)
- Matilda Neutzling (1889 – 1940)
- Carrie Neutzling (1899 – 1980)
- Louis Clifford Serig (1900 – 1977)
- Leah Serig (1903 – 1995)
- Helen Serig (1904 – 1988)

As discussed in this chapter, those seven had twenty-six children, Augustus Serig's 2x great-grandchildren. Those twenty-six are discussed in detail in Chapter X.

Relation to the Henry Line

This chapter discussed seven individuals from the third generation of the Augustus line who remained in the Wheeling area. The previous chapter discussed their third cousins, six individuals from the third generation of the Henry line who remained in the Wheeling area. These thirteen individuals were born between 1886 and 1914. In this section I examine where these families lived in relation to each other in 1940 when the thirteen descendants ranged in age from 26 to 54 years old.

In 1940 these thirteen individuals were scattered around the Wheeling area. However, there were two places in Wheeling in which members of both lines of the Serig family were living somewhat close to each other. Recall that Chapter VI concluded that in 1910 the best chance for a connection between the two lines of the Serig family was on Wheeling Island, where second cousins, Albert Serig, Jr. from the second generation of the Henry line, and Caroline Neutzling (nee Harding) from the second generation of the Augustus line, lived within a half mile of each other.

In 1940, Albert Serig, Jr. from the Henry line was living at 309 South Penn Street on Wheeling Island, just south of the current route of Interstate 70, along with his wife and their two children, Mary Kathleen and her younger brother, Jack. Albert's older brother, William, was living a four-minute walk away, at 67 Ohio Street. Throughout this period, his daughter Virginia and her husband Carl Neer lived with him.

From the Augustus line, Carrie Allen (nee Neutzling) and her husband, Fred, were living at 14 North Wabash Street on Wheeling Island, near her second cousins once removed, Albert and William. She was only a ten-minute walk from William and a twelve-minute walk from Albert.

The extent to which any of these increasingly distant cousins knew each other and were aware of their family connection is impossible to determine. Virginia Neer and Carrie Allen were both forty-one in 1940, but their different last names made a connection less obvious. On the other hand, although Mary Kathleen Serig and Jack Serig were considerably younger, only 26 and 23, respectively, but their last name of Serig was the same as Carrie's grandmother and uncle. Also, their parents, second cousins, had lived in the same general area for some years. These similarities suggest the possibility of a connection.

Another place where members of both lines of the Serig family lived somewhat close to each other was in South Wheeling. From the Henry line, Sara Schultze (nee Serig) was living at 3318 Eoff Street in 1940 with her younger son, Clarence, and her older son, William, and his family.

From the Augustus line, three of Louis August Serig's children were living close to his second cousin, Sara. Leah Ries (nee Serig) and her family were at 2627 Jacob Street in 1940. Helen Dueker (nee Serig) and her family were at 2518 Chapline Street in 1940. Louis Clifford Serig, was living at 2717 Jacob Street in 1934, and likely remained there until moving to Portsmouth City, Virginia shortly before the 1940 census. These three siblings were less than a five-minute walk from each other, and they all were less than a fifteen-minute walk from their second cousin once removed, Sara, and her sons, Clarence and William, their third cousins.

Again, the extent to which any of these distant cousins were aware of their family connection is impossible to determine. Louis Serig's' children, Louis (39), Leah (38), and Helen (36) were similar in age to their third cousins, Sara's sons, William (37) and Clarence, (34). However, among the five third cousins, only Louis had the last name Serig, making a family relationship less obvious.

Chapter IX
Fourth Generation – Henry Line

As discussed in Chapter VII, Henry E. Serig (1809 – 1851) had six great-grandchildren who remained in the Wheeling area and who together gave him twelve 2x great-grandchildren.

In the family tree below, I have removed Henry E. Serig's seven great-grandchildren who did not raise families in the Wheeling area, and I have added his twelve 2x great-grandchildren, the fourth American-born generation in the Henry line and the subject of this chapter.

As discussed below, seven of these twelve 2x great-grandchildren contributed to the fifth American-born generation of the Henry line in the Wheeling area. The spouses and ancestors for these seven are included in the family tree below. The other five either moved from the area (two) or I was not able to find information about them (three).

The Children of
Henry Bell (1902 – 1975) and Katharine Flannagan (1903 – 1983)

Jean Bell (1928 – 2006) was born on April 12, 1928 in Pittsburgh. She married Richard Brindley in 1949, and they divorced in 1984. She died in Norfolk, Virginia in 2006. She did not have children who lived in Wheeling.

Eleanor Bell (1935 – 2015) was born on November 6, 1935 in Wheeling. She married William Radar Dod in 1955. William was the owner of Dod Oil Co. in Staunton, Virginia and vice president of Outer Banks Video Cable TV, Inc., a business he started with his brother-in-law, Richard Brindley. Eleanor died in Lexington, Virginia in 2015. She did not have children who lived in Wheeling.

The Child of
Charles Louis Serig (1901 – 1981) and Wilma King (1900 – 1983)

James Louis Serig (1929 – 1992) was born on May 25, 1929 in Wheeling. He attended Triadelphia High School, and married Bonnie J.

Jewell (1925 – 2014) in 1951 in Belmont County, Ohio, across the river from Wheeling. James served in the Army from April 1951 to April 1953. After he returned from the army, James and Bonnie had two sons, Kent (1955) and Dean (1959). They are members of the fifth generation of the Henry line and are discussed further in Chapter XI. James died in Florida in 1992, at the age of 62. His obituary states that he moved to central Florida in 1990. Bonnie died in 2014 at the age of 89. They are both buried in the Chapel Hill Cemetery in Orlando, Florida.

Henry E. Serig Family Tree

Henry E. Serig (1809 – 1851) m: Mary Christina Dipple (1813 – 1888)

- Louis August Serig (1843 – 1923) m: Sarah Ann Lewellen (1848 – 1927) in 1868
  - George August Serig (1871 – 1956) m: Maud Cotts (1877 – 1923) in 1899
    - Charles Louis Serig (1901 – 1981) m: Wilma King (1900 – 1983) in 1922
      - James L. Serig (1929) married Bonnie J. Jewell (1925 – 2014) in 1951
  - Harry Newton Serig (1883 – 1954) m: Mary Lynch (1888 – 1947) in 1909
    - Harold Serig (1909 – 1952) m: Gertrude Foran Bartollas (1909 – 1982) in 1935
      - Patricia C. Serig (1936 –) m: Warren McKeen (1934 –) in 1957
      - Mary Ann Serig (1940 – 2011) m: John Gray (1934 – 1968) in 1960
    - Anna Catherine Serig (1911 – 185) m: John McMullen (1897 – 1968) in 1938
      - Joseph McMullen (1940 –) m: Carol Buzas (1941 – 2003) in 1961
      - Mary E. McMullen (1945 – 2018) m: Richard Metzger (1937-) in 1964
      - Sally McMullen (? – ?)
- Arthur Serig (1845 – 1921) m: Sarah Virginia Sykes (1849 – 1944) in 1867
  - Sara Serig (1878 – 1970) m: August Schultze (1877 – 1924) in 1901
    - William Schultze (1903 – 1979) m: Emma King (1908 – 1994) in 1925
      - Dorothy Schultze (1925)
      - Ilene Schultze (1931) m: Wallace Mann (1931 – 2008) in 1955
  - Albert Serig Jr. (1880 – 1965) m: Anna Mary Schultze (1880 – 1968) in 1906
    - Mary Kathleen Serig (1914 – 2009) m: Robert Muldoon (1916 – 1996)
      - Sally Muldoon (1950 –) m: Roland Habig (1951 –)
      - Robert Muldoon (1957)

The Children of
Harold Serig (1909 – 1952) and Gertrude Foran (1909 – 1982)

Patricia Catherine Serig (1936 –) was born on March 17, 1936. She married Warren James McKeen (1934 –) in 1957. An internet search indicates that Patricia and her husband are living in Bethany, West Virginia, about 17 miles northeast of Wheeling. Patricia's sister's obituary (see Mary Ann below) mentions being survived by two nephews and one niece, who are likely Patricia and Warren's children, but the obituary does not name them. One appears to be Warren James McKeen, Jr. (1959), who currently lives in Harrisonburg, Virginia, and is married to Elizabeth Anne Barnes, his second marriage. I have not been able to locate his two sisters.

Mary Ann Serig (1940 – 2011) was born on October 21, 1940. She married John Gray (1934 – 1968) in 1960, and they had three children, James (1960), Denise (1967), and John (?). John Gray (the father) died in 1967, one day after his 34th birthday. He served in the Army during the Korean War from September 1951 to September 1954, and is buried in the Riverview Cemetery in Moundsville, West Virginia. Mary Ann subsequently married Elwood Roth. He died in 1990. Mary Ann died in Iowa in 2011 at the age of 70. She is buried in the Mount Calvary Cemetery in Wheeling. At the time of Mary's death, her three children lived in Texas, Tennessee, and Iowa.

The Children of
Anna C. Serig (1911 – 1985) and John McMullen (1897 – 1968)

Joseph Newton McMullen (1940 –) was born on October 30, 1940. He married Carol Buzas (1941 – 2003) in 1961. They had two children, Renee (1963) and Joseph M. (1967), who are members of the fifth generation of the Henry line, and are discussed further in Chapter XI. Joseph's wife, Carol, died in 2003 at the age of 61. I cannot find where she is buried. An internet search shows that Joseph (the father) is living in Moundsville.

Mary Emily McMullen (1945 – 2018) was born on February 14, 1945. She married Richard Metzger (1937 –) in 1964. Mary Emily died in 2018 at the age of 73. She is buried in the Greenwood Cemetery in Wheeling. Her obituary does not mention her husband, Richard, who is still alive and living in Wheeling. Her obituary also does not mention siblings, whether surviving or having predeceased her. Her obituary says that she has two surviving children, Deanna (now Rush), married to Chuck Rush and living in Mooresville, North Carolina, and Richard, married to Tara McGinley and living in Cincinnati.

Sally McMullen (? – ?). I cannot find information about Sally.

The Children of
William Schultze (1903 – 1979) and Emma King (1908 – 1994)

Dorothy Schultze (1925 –) was born on August 25, 1925. In the 1940 census she was living with her parents and her sister at 3318 Eoff Street. Also at that address were her grandmother, Sara Schultze, and her uncle Clarence Schultze. In 1984 she was still living at 3318 Eoff Street in Wheeling. An internet search indicates that she is still living in Wheeling, and still with the last name Schultze. I cannot find any information indicating that she ever married or had children.

Ilene May Schultze (1931 – 2003) was born on May 23, 1931 in Wheeling. In the 1940 census she was living with her parents and her sister at 3318 Eoff Street. Also at that address were her grandmother, Sara Schultze, and her uncle Clarence Schultze. She married Wallace Harry Mann (1931 – 2008) in 1955 in Ohio County, West Virginia. They had four children, Richard (1954), Linda (1956), Douglas Alan (1960), and Thomas (1963). These four members of the fifth generation of the Henry line are discussed further in Chapter XI. Ilene died in 2003, at the age of 72, while living on North Erie Street in Wheeling. I could not locate where she is buried. Her obituary makes no mention of her (still living at that time) husband, Wallace. Other records indicate he was living in West Palm Beach, Florida in 1996, so he and Ilene may have been separated or divorced before that. Wallace died in 2008 when he was living in Fort Lauderdale, Florida.

The Children of
Mary K. Serig (1914 – 2009) and Robert Muldoon (1916 – 1996)

Sally Muldoon was born on June 11, 1950. She married Roland Habig (1951 –). They have two children, Ronald (1979) and Brian (1982), who are in the fifth generation of the Henry line, and are discussed further in Chapter XI. Sally's father-in-law died in 2009, and according to his obituary Sally and Ron Habig were living in St. Clairsville, Ohio, across the Ohio River, 11 miles from Wheeling. An internet search indicates that Sally and Roland still live in St. Clairsville.

Robert Muldoon was born on March 14, 1957. An internet search indicates that he still lives in Wheeling. I cannot find any information that he is or has been married or has children.

Summary

Seven of Henry E. Serig's 2x great-grandchildren, the fourth generation in the Henry line, raised their families in the Wheeling area.

- James Louis Serig (1929 – 1992)
- Patricia Catherine Serig (1936 –)
- Mary Ann Serig (1940 – 2011)
- Joseph N. McMullen (1940 –)
- Mary Emily McMullen (1945 – 2018)
- Ilene May Schultze (1931 – 2003)
- Sally Muldoon (1950 –)

As discussed in this chapter, those seven had eighteen children, Henry E. Serig's 3x great-grandchildren, who are discussed further in Chapter XI.

Chapter X
Fourth Generation – Augustus Line

As discussed in Chapter VIII, Augustus Serig (1809 – 1851) had seven great-grandchildren who raised families in the Wheeling area. These seven great-grandchildren gave him twenty-six 2x great-grandchildren

As previously, I have removed from the family tree below Augustus' eleven great-grandchildren who did not raise children in the Wheeling area, and I have added his twenty-six 2x great-grandchildren, the fourth generation in the Augustus line and the subject of this chapter.

As discussed below, only five of these twenty-six 2x great-grandchildren contributed to the fifth generation of the Henry line in the Wheeling area. The spouses and ancestors for these five are included in the family tree below. The other twenty-one either died young (three), lived to be an adult but never had children (five), or moved away from the Wheeling area (thirteen).

The Children of
Carrie Moore (1891 – 1981) and Ralph Woods (1890 – 1955)

Henrietta Moore Woods (1913 – 1991) was born on May 23, 1913 in Bridgeport, Ohio, across the river from Wheeling. She married Carl William Glitsch (1912 – 1979) in 1934 and they had one child, Marjorie Lee (1938), a fifth-generation descendant of Augustus, who is discussed further in Chapter XII. In 1940, Henrietta, Carl, and Marjorie were living in Pease, Ohio, across the river and about seven miles north of Wheeling. Carl was working as a motorman for the transit company. Carl died in 1974 at the age of 67, and Henrietta died in 1991 at the age of 77. They are both buried in the Belmont County Memorial Park.

Ralph Van Woods, Jr. (1916 – 1988) was born on February 4, 1916 in Wheeling. He married Jane Ruth Weber (1919 – 2008) in 1943 in Tucson, Arizona, when he was in training as a crew chief on the B-17 bombers. After the war they moved to the Dallas-Fort Worth area where they spent the rest of their lives. They had three children, two sons, Dale and Dan, and a daughter, Nancy. None of the children returned to live in Wheeling.

Augustus Serig Family Tree

Augustus Serig (1812 – 1862) m: Sophia Mary Elizabeth (1813 – 1888) about 1839

- Matilda Serig (1845 – 1892) m: Louis Harding (1840 – 1869)
  - Elizabeth Serig (1864 – 1943) m: John Louis Moore (1863 – 1933) in 1888
    - Carrie Moore (1891 – 1981) m: Ralph Woods (1890 -1955) in 1912
      - Henrietta Woods (1913 – 1991) m: Carl Glitsch (1912 – 1979) in 1934
      - Ralph Woods (1916 – 1988)
      - Marjorie Woods (1919 – 1920)
  - Caroline Harding (1868 – 1954) m: Peter Nuetzling (1862 – 1927) in 1884
    - Elmer Neutzling (1888 – 1956) m: Myrtle Williams (1886 – 1974) in 1907
      - Madolyn (1909 – 2005)
      - Leona Neutzling (1910 – 1989)
      - Janice Neutzling (1913 – 1925)
      - Eleanor Neutzling (1914 – 2005)
      - Elmer Neutzling (1919 – 1995)
      - Rosalie Neutzling (1921 – 2010)
    - Matilda Neutzling (1889 – 1940) m: Gomer Liston (1888 – 1964) in 1908
      - Gomer Liston (1911 – 1983) m: Ella Allen (1909 – 1962) in 1936
      - Vernon Liston (1912 – 1995)
    - Carrie Neutzling (1899 – 1980)
      - Guy Allen (1917 – 2017)
      - Matilda Allen (1918 – 2000)
      - Carl Allen (1925 – 2008)
      - Glen Allen (1927 – 1993)
  - Louis August Serig (1871 – 1946) m: Amelia Eberling (1874 – 1923) in 1893
    - Louis Clifford Serig (1900 – 1977) m: Loma Ward (1901 – 1938) in 1921
      - Louis Serig (1922 – 1923)
      - Charles Serig (1923 – 2003) m: Ruth Klinkler (1924 – 2007) in 1945
      - Jack Serig (1928 – 2014)
      - Ward Serig (1933 –)
      - Joe Serig (1935 – 2018)
    - Leah A Serig (1902 – 1995) m: George Ries (1896 – 1974) in 1921
      - George Ries (1925 – 1987) m: Mary Goodman (nee Burger) (1931 – 2017) in 1955
      - Glen Ries (1928 – 2007) m: Norma Jeanne Cecil (1932 – 1955) in 1949
      - Kathryn Ries (1934 – 2015)

Marjorie Woods (1919 – 1920) was born on February 15, 1919. She died at the age of 21 months in 1920. She is buried in the Greenwood Cemetery.

The Children of
Elmer Neutzling (1886 – 1956) and Myrtle Williams (1886 – 1974)

Madolyn Dorothy Neutzling (1909 – 2005) was born on January 31, 1909. She married William Wesley Lowery (1908 – 1976) in 1930. They had two sons, James Edward (1933) and William Rockne (1934). William's World War II draft card indicates that he and Madolyn were living in Warren, Ohio, about 100 miles north of Wheeling. William died in 1976 at the age of 68, and Madolyn died in 2005, at the age of 96, both in Warren. It appears their children did not return to live in Wheeling.

Leona Neutzling (1910 – 1989) was born on December 2, 1910 in Wheeling. She married Norman Keesecker (1909 – 1979) in 1929 in Martinsburg, West Virginia, about 230 miles east of Wheeling. They had two children, Margaret Ann (1933) and Thomas (1937). Norman died in 1979 at the age of 70, and Leona died in 1989, at the age of 78. They are both buried in Rosedale Cemetery in Martinsburg. It appears that neither child returned to live in the Wheeling area.

Janice Neutzling (1913 – 1925) was born on March 28, 1913 in Wheeling. She died in 1925 at the age of 12 in Follansbee, West Virginia, about 25 miles north of Wheeling.

Eleanor Neutzling (1914 – 2005) was born on November 23, 1914 in Bridgeport, Ohio, across the river from Wheeling. She married John Pool (1909 – 1980) in 1933. In 1940, the family was living in Warren, Ohio, about 100 miles north of Wheeling. John was working in a steel mill. Eleanor's sister, Madolyn, and her husband were also living in Warren. John died in 1980 at the age of 71, and Eleanor died in 2005 at the age of 90, both in the Warren area. They had two sons, John (1934) and Robert (1947), neither of whom returned to live in the Wheeling area.

Elmer Sydney Neutzling (1919 – 1995) was born on February 21, 1919 in Wheeling. He married Helen Louise Scott (1917 – 1961) in 1940 in Wheeling. They had three children, Ray William (1934), Gayle Louise (1942), and Homer (1946). According to Elmer's World War II draft registration card, Elmer and Helen were living at 2745 Wood Street in Wheeling. By 1952, the family had moved to Canton, Ohio. They were still there in 1993. Helen died in 1961 at the age of 44, and Elmer died in 1995 at the age of 76, both in Canton. The children grew up in Canton, and did not return to live in the Wheeling area.

Rosalie Neutzling (1921 – 2010) was born on June 7, 1921. By 1938 she had moved to Warren, Ohio, where she lived for the rest of her life. Rosalie died in Warren in 2010 at the age of 89. It appears that she never married.

The Children of
Matilda Neutzling (1889 – 1940) and Gomer Liston (1888 – 1964)

Gomer Paul Liston (1911 – 1983) was born on June 2, 1911 in Wheeling. He married Ella Louise Allen (1909 – 1962) in 1936 in Wheeling. They had one daughter Carol Lee (1937). In 1940 the family was living with Gomer's parents in Bridgeport across the river from Wheeling, and Gomer was working as a laborer in a steel mill. Gomer's wife, Ella, died in 1962 at the age of 53, and is buried in the Belmont County Memorial Park in Saint Clairsville, Ohio. Gomer died in 1983 at the age of 72 in Bridgeport. I cannot find any more information about their daughter, Carol Lee Liston.

Vernon Matthew Liston (1912-95) was born on December 17, 1912 in Wheeling. He married Vivian Faye Blackwell (1917 – 1991) in 1940, and they were divorced in 1970. It appears that they did not have any children. Vernon died in Bellaire, Ohio in 1995 at the age of 82.

The Children of
Carrie Neutzling and Fred Allen (1888 – 1974)

Guy Peter Allen (1917 – 2017) was born on March 19, 1917 in Wheeling. He married Shirley Griffin (1919 – 1985) (not sure of last name or year of marriage). They had two children, Peter G. and Pamela. Shirley died in 1985 at the age of 66, and Guy died in 2017 at the age of 100. Both are buried in the First Reformed Church Cemetery in Pompton Plains, New Jersey, 115 miles northeast of Philadelphia. I cannot find any information on the children, Peter and Pamela, but it is unlikely they returned to live in the Wheeling area.

Matilda Ruth Allen (1918-2000) was born on November 15, 1918 in Wheeling. She was likely named after her aunt and/or her grandmother, both named Matilda. She married Charles Stevenson (1902 – 1979) in 1939 in Bridgeport, Ohio. Charles died in 1979 at the age of 75, and

Matilda died in 2000 at the age of 81, both in Magnolia, Ohio, about 65 miles northwest of Wheeling. They are both buried in the Magnolia Cemetery. It appears that they did not have any children.

Carl David Allen (1925-2008) was born on October 6, 1925 in Wheeling. He married Sherolyn Fisher (1939 – 2020) in 1962 in Wheeling. At the time of Carl's World War II draft registration card, he was living in Wheeling and working at the Bolten Cigar Store on Market Street. He served in the Army from February 1944 to August 1945. It appears that Carl and Sherolyn moved to Florida in the late 1980s. Carl died in 2008 at the age of 82, and his last address was in Sarasota, Florida. Sherolyn died in Franklin, North Carolina in 2020 at the age of 82. It appears that they did not have any children.

Glen Richard Allen (1927-93) was born on November 16, 1927 in Wheeling. He married Mary Elizabeth Brown (1905 – 1988) in 1951. Glen died in 1993, at the age of 65, in Tappahannock, Virginia, about 50 miles northeast of Richmond. I cannot find any more information on Mary or whether they had children.

<h3 align="center">The Children of
Louis Serig (1900 – 1977) and Loma Ward (1901 – 1938)</h3>

Louis Albert Serig (1922 – 1923) was born on June 13, 1922 and died on July 13, 1923 at the age of thirteen months. He is buried in the Greenwood Cemetery in Wheeling.

Charles Edward Serig (1922 – 2003) was born on November 9, 1923. He married Ruth Klinkler (1924 – 2007) in 1945 in Wheeling. They had three children, Janet (1947), and twins, Karen and Kevin (1955). Details on this family are provided in Chapter XIII.

Jack William Serig (1928 – 2014) was born on August 3, 1928 in Wheeling. Jack married Lourdes Hernandez (1933 – 2021) in Cuba in 1950. They had five children, Arthur Lewis (1954), Jack Jr. (1959), Charles Edward (1960), Shawna (1964), and Kendrick Allen (1966). Details on this family are provided in Chapter XIV.

Ward Earl Kendrick Serig (1933 –) was born on October 2, 1933 in Wheeling. He married Donnie Merle Smith (1933 –) in 1955. They had four children, Steven Allen (1957), Joy Loma (1958), Kendrick Allen

(1963), and Julie Elizabeth (1969). Details on this family are provided in Chapter XIV.

Joe Allen Serig (1935 – 2018) was born on April 18, 1935. He married Beverly Wilson (1934 -) in 1955. They had four children, Deborah Joan (1958), Marjorie Ellen (1960), Craig Bernard (1962), and Daniel Allen (1969). Details on this family are provided in Chapter XIV.

The Children of
Leah Serig (1902 – 1995) and George Ries (1896 – 1974)

George Harold Ries (1925 – 1987) was born on September 18, 1925 in Wheeling. He married Mary Elizabeth Goodman (nee Burger) (1931 – 2017) in 1955 and they had three children, Leah Ann (1955), Lynn Ellen (1958), and Barbara Sue (1960). The children are fifth generation descendants of Augustus, and are discussed in detail in Chapter XII. George served in the Army from October 1943 to March 1946, and again from August 1950 to August 1951. He died in St. Clairsville, Ohio in 1987 at the age of 61. Mary died in Wheeling in 2017 at the age of 86, and is buried in the Greenwood Cemetery in Wheeling along with other members of the Burger family.

Glenn Robert Ries (1928 – 2007) was born on June 19, 1928 in Wheeling. He married Norma Jeanne Cecil (1932 – 1955) in 1949. They had two surviving children, Cheryl Anne (1951) and Thomas M. (1952). Their third child, Ellen Sue (1953), died the day after her birth, and is buried in the Greenwood Cemetery. Norma Jeanne died in 1955 at the age of 22, and is buried in the Greenwood Cemetery. Later that year Glenn married Karen Mae Lowe, and they had two children, David (1956) and Evelyn (1957). All four of Glenn's surviving children are fifth generation descendants of Augustus and are discussed further in Chapter XII. Glenn died in Jacksonville, Florida in 2007, at the age of 78, and is buried in the Greenwood Cemetery in Wheeling. I cannot find more information about Glenn's second wife, Karen.

Kathryn June Ries (1934 – 2015) was born on June 1, 1934 in Wheeling. She married Ray Charles Dodds (1927 –) in 1956 in Wheeling. They had four children, Brenda Kay (1961), Steven Ray (1959), Charles Brian (1957), and Jeanne Marie (1955). At some point, Kathryn and Ray moved to Independence, Missouri where Ray was an official in the Reorganized Church of Jesus Christ of the Latter Day Saints. However, in the mid

1980's the church authorized the ordination of women and Kathryn and Ray left the church over the issue. Kathryn died in Lees Summit, Missouri in 2015, at the age of 80. An internet search shows that Ray Dodds is still living in Independence and is 93 years old. None of the children returned to live in the Wheeling area.

The Children of
Helen Serig (1904 – 1988) and Charles Dueker (1899 – 1965)

Lois I. Dueker (1926 -) was born in 1926 (I cannot find the exact date). Her mother's obituary in 1988 from the Kingsport, Tennessee *Times-News* says that she is survived by a daughter, Mrs. George (Lois) Robinson of Kingsport. Apparently, Helen followed Lois to Kingsport, Tennessee, about 400 miles south of Wheeling. I can't find further information on Lois.

Elizabeth Dueker (1928 – 2012) was born on December 23, 1928. She married Albert Charles Flanders in about 1954. Her mother's obituary in 1988 from the Kingsport, Tennessee *Times-News* says that she is survived by a daughter, Mrs. Albert (Elizabeth) Flanders of Texarkana, Arkansas. Elizabeth died in Wheeling in 2012, at the age of 83. Albert died in Cary, North Carolina, in 2015, at the age of 95. They are both buried in the Greenwood Cemetery. They had five children, Andrea, David, Edmund, Elaine, and Janet. I cannot find their birth years. Albert's obituary indicates that in 2015 Andrea lived in San Francisco, David lived in Rockville, Maryland, Edmund lived in Seattle, Elaine lived in Richmond, Virginia, and Janet lived in Apex, North Carolina. It is unlikely that any returned to live in the Wheeling area.

Richard Lee Dueker (1940 -) was born on June 14, 1940 in Wheeling. His mother's obituary in 1988 from the Kingsport, Tennessee *Times-News* says that she is survived by a son, Richard L. Dueker of Butler, Pennsylvania (north of Pittsburgh, about 100 miles from Wheeling). An internet search indicates that Richard is living in Florida, but I cannot find whether he had any children.

Summary

Five of Augustus Serig's 2x great-grandchildren, the fourth generation in the Augustus line, raised their families in the Wheeling area.

- Henrietta Woods (1913 – 1991)
- Gomer Liston (1911 – 1983)
- Charles Edward Serig (1923 – 2003)
- George Harold Ries (1925 – 1987)
- Glenn Robert Ries (1928 – 2007)

As discussed in this chapter, those five had thirteen children, Augustus Serig's 3x great-grandchildren. Ten of the thirteen are discussed in detail in Chapter XII. The three children of Charles Serig are discussed in detail Chapter XIII.

Relation to the Henry Line

This chapter discussed five individuals from the fourth generation of the Augustus line who remained in the Wheeling area. The previous chapter discussed their fourth cousins, seven individuals from the fourth generation of the Henry line who remained in the Wheeling area.

These twelve individuals were born between 1911 and 1950. The most recent available census data is for 1940, at which time the oldest of these individuals was 29, and some of them were yet to be born. Finding information about these individuals after the 1940 census is much more difficult.

Chapter VIII described two locations in Wheeling where there were possible connections between members of the Henry line of the Serig family and members of the Augustus line.

The first was on Wheeling Island where Carrie Allen (nee Neutzling) from the Augustus line was living relatively close to three of her third cousins from the Henry line. However, only one of these four individuals had a child who remained in the Wheeling area. That child was Sally Habig (nee Muldoon), daughter of Mary Kathleen Serig and Robert Muldoon, and a fourth-generation descendant in the Henry line. Sally still lives in the Wheeling area, as discussed in Chapter IX. This does not suggest a continuing connection with the Augustus side of the family.

The second location was in South Wheeling where Clarence and William Schultze from the Henry line were living about a fifteen-minute walk from three of their third cousins from the Augustus line, siblings Louis Serig, Leah Ries (nee Serig), and Helen Dueker (nee Serig).

From the Henry line, Clarence Schultze did not have any children. His brother, William, had two daughters, Dorothy and Ilene, both fourth generation descendants of Henry. An internet search indicates that Dorothy is alive and still living in Wheeling, but that she likely never married or had children. Internet searches also indicate that descendants of Dorothy's siter, Ilene, are still living in the Wheeling area. Those descendants are discussed further in Chapter XI.

From the Augustus line, only Leah's children, George and Glenn Ries, remained in the Wheeling area. They are both fourth generation descendants of Augustus, and their children are discussed further in Chapter XII.

Thus, the only potential continuing connection between the two lines of the Serig family based on physical proximity is between descendants of Leah Ries (nee Serig) and descendants of Ilene Mann (nee Schultze). And this is based only on the slim evidence that Leah lived about a fifteen-minute walk from Ilene in the 1930s. However, Leah was much older than Ilene. In 1940, Leah turned 37 while Ilene only turned nine. Slim evidence of a connection, indeed.

There is one more individual worth mentioning who is discussed further in the final chapter, John "Jack" Serig (1917 – 2004), Mary Kathleen Muldoon's (nee Serig) brother and Sally Habig's uncle. Jack was a third generation descendant in the Henry line. In 1940, Jack was about 23 years old and living with his sister and parents on Wheeling Island at 309 South Penn Street. Although he married twice, he did not have any children. On the other hand, he was highly visible in Wheeling society and likely was known by contemporary members of the Augustus line of the Serig family.

Chapter XI
Fifth and Sixth Generations – Henry Line

As discussed in Chapter IX, Henry E. Serig (1809 – 1851) had seven 2x great-grandchildren who remained in the Wheeling area and who together gave him eighteen 3x great-grandchildren. In the family tree below, I have removed Henry E. Serig's five 2x great-grandchildren who did not raise their families in the Wheeling area, and I have added his eighteen 3x great-grandchildren, the fifth generation in the Henry line.

Six of the eighteen 3x great-grandchildren remained in the Wheeling area to raise their families. The spouses and ancestors for these six are included in the family tree below. The other twelve either moved from the area (ten) or I was not able to find information about them (two). The six who remained in the Wheeling area had seven children, members of the sixth generation in the Henry line, and Henry's 4x great-grandchildren. Six of these seven still live in the Wheeling area. These six are described below, but have not been added to the family tree.

The Children of
James Serig (1929 – 1992) and Bonnie Jewell (1925 – 2014)

Kent Robert Serig (1956 –) was born on March 17, 1955. He graduated from high school in St. Clairsville in 1974, and married Manetta K. Gooch (1959 –) in 1979. Public records indicate that he has lived in the greater Orlando, Florida area since 1988. An internet search indicates that Kent is living in Castleberry, Florida, near Orlando, that Manetta is living in Mount Dora, Florida, about thirty miles away, and that they have a daughter, Cristina Leigh Serig (1980), who also lives in Florida.

Dean Serig (1959 –) was born on September 16, 1959. He married Maria Lynn Frankovich (1965) in 1990. An internet search indicates that he and Maria currently live in Dillonvale, Ohio, about 20 miles north of Wheeling. It also appears that they have a son, Robert Henderson Serig (1987), who also lives in Dillonvale, at the same address, and may be married. Robert is a member of the sixth generation of the Henry line.

Henry E. Serig Family Tree

Henry E. Serig (1809 – 1851) m: Mary Christina Dipple (1813 – 1888)

- Louis August Serig (1843 – 1923) m: Mary Christina Dipple (1813 – 1888) in 1868
  - George August Serig (1871 – 1956) m: Maud Cotts (1877 – 1923) in 1899
    - Charles L. Serig (1901 – 1981) m: Wilma King ((1900 – 1983) in 1922
      - James L. Serig (1929) m: Bonnie Jewell (1925 – 2014) in 1951
        - Kent Serig (1955)
        - Dean Serig (1959) m: Maria Frankovich (1965) in 1990
  - Harry Newton Serig (1883 – 1954) m: Mary Lynch (1888 – 1947) in 1909
    - Harold Serig (1909 – 1952) m: Gertrude Bartollas (1909 – 1982) in 1935
      - Patricia C. Serig (1936) m: Warren McKeen (1934 –) in 1957
        - Warren McKeen, Jr. (1959 –)
        - Unknown Daughter
        - Unknown Son
      - Mary Ann Serig (1940 – 2011) m: John Gray (1934 – 1968) in 1960
        - James Gray (1960 –)
        - Denise Gray (1967 –)
        - John Gray (? –)
    - Anna C. Serig (1911 – 1985) m: John McMullen (1897 – 1968) in 1938
      - Joseph N. McMullen (1940 –) m: Carol Buzas in 1961
        - Renee McMullen (1963 –)
        - Joseph M. McMullen (1967 –) m: Susan Black (1966 –)
- Arthur Serig (1845 – 1921) m: Sarah Virginia Sykes (1849 – 1944) in 1867
  - Sara Serig (1878 – 1970) m: August Schultze (1877 – 1924) in 1901
    - William Schultze (1903 – 1979) m: Emma King (1908 – 1994) in 1925
      - Ilene Schultze (1931 – 2003) m: Wallace Mann (1931 – 2008) in 1955
        - Richard Mann (1954 –)
        - Linda Mann (1956 –) m: Mark Kaminski (1958 –)
        - Douglas Alan Mann (1960 –)
        - Thomas Mann (1963 –) m: Teresa Riggs (19xx –)
  - Albert Serig Jr. (1880 – 1965) m: Anna M. Schultze (1880 – 1968) in 1906
    - Mary K. Serig (1914 – 2009) m: Robert Muldoon (1916 – 1996)
      - Sally Muldoon (1950 –) m: Roland Habig (1951 –)
        - Ronald Habig (1979 –) m: Fallon Kendra Namack (1987 –)
        - Brian Habig (1982 –) m: Elizabeth Connell (1980 –) in 2006

The Children of
Patricia Catherine Serig (1936 –) and James McKeen (1934 –)

Warren James McKeen, Jr. (1959 –) currently lives in Harrisonburg, Virginia, and is married to Elizabeth Anne Barnes, his second marriage.

Unknown Daughter – I cannot find any information about this person.

Unknown Son – I cannot find any information about this person.

The Children of
Mary Ann Serig (1940 – 2011) and John Gray (1934 – 1968)

James Gray (1960 –) was born on December 12, 1960. An internet search shows that James currently lives in Texas.

Denise Gray (1967 –) was born on December 31, 1967. An internet search shows that Denise currently lives in Iowa.

John Gray (? –) I cannot locate any information about John.

The Children of
Joseph N. McMullen (1940 –) and Carol Buzas (1941 – 2003)

Renee M. McMullen (1963 –) was born on May 28, 1963. She married James Woodrum (1961 –), year unknown. In 2003, at the time of her mother's death, Renee and James were living in Winfield, West Virginia (about 160 miles south of Wheeling). An internet search shows that Renee and James are still living in Winfield, although at different addresses.

Joseph M. McMullen (1967 –) was born on November 10, 1967. He married Susan Black (1966 –), year unknown. They were living in Moundsville in 2003 at the time of his mother's death. An internet search shows that Joseph and Susan still live in Moundsville.

The Children of
Mary McMullen (1945 – 2018) and Richard Metzger (1937 –)

Richard Metzger (1965 –) was born on October 25, 1965. At the time of his mother's death in 2018, Richard was married to Tara McGinley and living in Cincinnati. An internet search shows that he still lives in Cincinnati.

Deanna Metzger (1967 –) was born on July 21, 1967. She married Mark Wayne in 1992, and they divorced in 2009. At the time of her mother's death in 2018, Deanna was married to Chuck Rush and living in Mooresville, North Carolina. An internet search shows that she still lives in Mooresville, North Carolina.

The Children of
Ilene May Schultze (1931 – 2003) and Wallace Mann (1931 – 2008)

Richard Mann (1954 –) was born on May 30, 1954 in West Palm Beach Florida. He married Diana Lynn Hay in 1990 in Florida. At the time of his mother's death in 2003, Richard was living in West Palm Beach, Florida with his wife Diana. An internet search indicates that they currently live in Port Saint Lucie, Florida.

Linda Mann (1956 –) was born on October 13, 1956 in Wheeling. She married Mark Kaminski (1958), year unknown. They had two children, Kerrie Ann (1992) and Markie Lin (1993), who are members of the sixth generation of the Henry line. An internet search indicates that Linda and Mark and their daughter, Kerrie Ann, still live in Wheeling, and that Markie Lin either lives in St. Clairsville or in Mount Washington, Pennsylvania, about 60 miles northeast of Wheeling.

Douglas Alan Mann (1960 – 2015) was born on June 20, 1960 in Wheeling. He married Christine Ann Joyce (1961) in Las Vegas in 1979. They had three children, Bethany Nicole (1988), Nicholas Tyler (1991), and Nathan (?). Douglas died in 2015 in Columbus, Ohio. Records indicate that he was divorced at the time of his death. Internet searches indicate that Bethany and Nicholas live in Columbus, Ohio and that Nathan lives in Westerville, Ohio, about 15 miles north of Columbus.

Thomas Mann (1963 – 2005) was born on August 7, 1963 in Wheeling. He married Teresa Riggs. Teresa had a son from a previous marriage, Charles Riggs, who died in 2020 at the age of 45. Thomas and Teresa had four children, Jessica Ann (1986), Justin (1988), Morgan (1992), and Lindsey (1994). Thomas died in 2005 in Wheeling at the age of 41. His son, Justin, died in 2019 at the age of 30. An internet search indicates that Jessica and Morgan live in Wheeling, and that Lindsey lives in St. Clairsville, Ohio. They are all members of the sixth generation of the Henry line.

The Children of
Sally Muldoon (1950 –) and Roland Habig (1951 –)

Ronald Habig (1979 –) was born on August 24, 1979. He is a member of the fifth generation of the Henry line. Ronald married Fallon Kendra Namack (1987), year unknown. An internet search indicates that Ronald and Fallon live in Wheeling.

Brian Habig (1982 –) was born on February 17, 1982. He is a member of the fifth generation of the Henry line. He married Elizabeth P. Connell in 2006. An internet search indicates that Brian lives in Bridgeport, Ohio and Elizabeth lives in Mason, Ohio, more than 200 miles southwest of Wheeling, so they are likely divorced.

Summary

Six of Henry E. Serig's eighteen 3x great-grandchildren, the fifth generation in the Henry line, raised their families in the Wheeling area.

- Dean Serig (1959 –)
- Joseph M. McMullen (1967 –)
- Linda Mann (1956 –)
- Thomas Mann (1963 – 2005)
- Ronald Habig (1979 –)
- Brian Habig (1982 –)

As discussed in this chapter, those six had seven children, Henry E. Serig's 4x great-grandchildren, one of whom is deceased. The other six still live in the Wheeling area, and are summarized in Chapter XV

- Robert Henderson Serig (1987 –)
- Kerrie Ann Kaminski (1992 –)
- Markie Lin Kaminski (1993 –)
- Jessica Ann Mann (1986 –)
- Morgan Mann (1992 –)
- Lindsey Mann (1994 –)

Chapter XII
Fifth and Sixth Generations – Augustus Line

As discussed in Chapter X, Augustus Serig (1812 – 1862) had five 2x great-grandchildren who remained in the Wheeling area, and are members of the fourth generation in the Augustus line. These five gave Augustus thirteen 3x great-grandchildren. In the family tree below, I have removed August Serig's twenty-one 2x great-grandchildren who did not raise their families in the Wheeling area, and I have added his thirteen 3x great-grandchildren, the fifth generation in the Augustus line.

Three of these thirteen are children of Charles Edward Serig. They are discussed in detail, along with their children and grandchildren, in Chapter XIII.

The other ten 3x great-grandchildren of Augustus are discussed in this chapter, along with their children and grandchildren. Two of these ten remained in the Wheeling area to raise their families. The spouses and ancestors for these two are included in the family tree below. The other eight either died young (one), moved from the area (four), or I was not able to find information about them (three). The two who remained in the Wheeling area had two children. These two are members of the sixth generation in the Augustus line, but both moved away from the Wheeling area, and are not included in the family tree.

The Children of
Henrietta Woods (1913 – 1991) and Carl Glitsch (1912 – 1979)

Marjorie Lee Glitsch (1938 –) was born on November 19, 1938. She married Gerald James Lofton (1939 –), and they had at least two sons, David James Lofton (1963) and Edward Carl Lofton (1967), who are sixth generation descendants of Augustus. Internet searches shows that Marjorie and Gerald live in Bridgeport, Ohio, across the river from Wheeling, that one son, Edward, lives in Cincinnati, and the other son, David, lives in North Carolina.

Augustus Serig Family Tree

Augustus Serig (1812 – 1862) m: Sophia Mary Elizabeth (1813 – 1888) about 1839

- Matilda Serig (1845 – 1892) m: Louis Harding (1840 – 1869)
  - Elizabeth Serig (1864 – 1943) m: John Louis Moore (1863 – 1933) in 1888
    - Carrie Moore (1891 – 1981) m: Ralph Woods (1890 -1955) in 1912
      - Henrietta (1913 – 1991) m: Carl Glitsch (1912 – 1979) in 1934
        - Marjorie Lee Glitsch (1938 –) m: Gerald Lofton (1939 –)
  - Louis August Serig (1871 – 1946) m: Amelia Eberling (1874 – 1923) in 1893
    - Louis Clifford Serig (1900 – 1977) m: Loma Ward (1901 – 1938) in 1921
      - Charles Serig (1923 – 2003)
        - Janet Serig (1947 –)
        - Karen Serig (1955 –)
        - Kevin Serig (1955 –)
      - Jack Serig (1928 – 2014)
      - Ward Serig (1933 –)
      - Joe Serig (1935 – 2018)
    - Leah A Serig (1902 – 1995) m: George Ries (1896 – 1974) in 1921
      - George Ries (1925 – 1987) m: Mary Burger (1931 – 2017) in 1955
        - Leah Anne Ries (1955 –)
        - Lynn Ries (1958 –)
        - Barbara Sue ("Suzie") Ries (1960 –) m: James Paknik (1957 –) in 1978; d: in 1980; m: Joseph Palmer (1957 –) in 1982; d: in 1991.
      - Glenn Ries (1928 – 2007) m: Norma Cecil (1932 – 1955) in 1949
        - Cheryl Anne Ries (1951 –)
        - Thomas Ries (1952 –)
        - Ellen Sue Ries (1953 – 1953)
      - Glenn Ries (1928 – 2007)
        - David Ries (1956 –)
        - Evelyn Ries (1957 –)

The Child of
Gomer Liston (1911 – 1983) and Ella Louise Allen (1909 – 1962)

Carol Lee Liston (1937 - ?) was born on October 19, 1937. I cannot find any additional information about Carol Lee.

The Children of
Charles Serig (1923 – 2003) and Ruth Klinkler (1924 – 2007)

Janet Ruth Serig (1947 –) was born on November 17, 1947 in Wheeling. Details about Janet and her descendants are provided in Chapter XIII.

Karen Sue Serig (1955 –) was born on March 30, 1955 in Wheeling. Details about Karen and her descendants are provided in Chapter XIII.

Kevin Allen Serig (1955 –) was born on March 30, 1955 in Wheeling. Details about Kevin and his descendants are provided in Chapter XIII.

The Children of
George Ries (1925 – 1987) and Mary Burger (1931 – 2017)

Leah Anne Ries (1955 – 1997) was born on September 26, 1955 in Steubenville, Ohio. She married John Patrick McGough (1954) in 1982, and they had one daughter, Elizabeth Alverta McGough (1982), that same year. They divorced in 1984. Leah Anne's social security application indicates that she was previously married to Irwin Emil Koegler (1956), and subsequently married to Doug Brown. Leah Anne died in 1997 at the age of 42 in Jackson County, West Virginia, about 130 miles southwest of Wheeling. Leah Anne's daughter, Elizabeth, married Benjamin Paul Bortner in 2002 in Norfolk, Virginia. They divorced in 2003. She married Eric Ray Pent in 2004 in Norfolk, and they divorced in 2008. She married Benjamin David Anderson in 2008 in Virginia Beach, Virginia.

Lynn Ellen Ries (1958 –) was born on September 17, 1958. She married Larry D. Puckett (1940 – 2020) in 1986, and they divorced in 1987. At the time of her mother's death in 2017, Lynn was living in North Carolina. An internet search shows a Lynn Worley with the same birthdate living in Richlands, North Carolina, and associated with Christopher Worley (1983), who may be her son.

Barbara Sue "Suzie" Ries (1960 –) was born on March 2, 1960. She married James H. Paknik in 1978, and they divorced in 1980. She married

Joseph H. Palmer in 1982, and they divorced in 1991. At the time of her mother's death in 2017, she was living in Dillonvale, Ohio, about 18 miles north of Wheeling. An internet search shows that she is still living in Dillonvale.

The Children of
Glenn Ries (1928 – 2007) and Norma Cecil (1932 – 1955)

Cheryl Anne Ries (1951 –) was born on April 1, 1951. She married Donald Eugene Coleman (1951 –) in 1968. They must have divorced because she married Kenneth Ray Canupp (1944 –) in 1973 in Richmond, Virginia. They divorced in 1981 in Carteret, North Carolina. That same day, in 1981, in the same place, Carteret, North Carolina, she married William Farrow Harvey (? – ?). She divorced William Harvey in 1996 in Clark County, Nevada (Las Vegas). I cannot find any additional information about Cheryl Anne.

Thomas M. Ries (1952 –) was born on March 5, 1952. He married Marjorie Rose Staub (1952) in 1971, and they were divorced in 1977. He married Joanne Miller (1958) in Winchester, Virginia in 1977. I cannot find any additional information about Thomas.

Ellen Sue Ries was born on March 30, 1955 and died on March 31, 1955, both in Wheeling. She is buried in the Greenwood Cemetery.

The Children of
Glenn Ries (1928 – 2007) and Karen Lowe (1936 –)

David Ries (1956 –) was born on July 16, 1956. I cannot find any additional information about David.

Evelyn Ries (1957 –) was born on October 16, 1957. I cannot find any additional information about Evelyn.

Summary

Four of Augustus Serig's thirteen 3x great-grandchildren, the fifth generation in the Augustus line, stayed in the Wheeling area. Two are discussed in this chapter.

- Marjorie Lee Lofton (1938 –)
- Barbara Sue "Suzie" Palmer (1960 –)

I cannot find any information that Marjorie or Suzie have children in the Wheeling area.

The other two are children of Charles Serig, and are discussed in detail in Chapter XIII.

- Janet Nixon (1947 –)
- Kevin Serig (1955 –)

All of the descendants of Augustus who are still living in the Wheeling area are summarized in Chapter XV.

Relation to the Henry Line

This chapter discussed four individuals from the fifth generation of the Augustus line who remained in the Wheeling area, and the four individuals from the sixth generation of the Augustus line who remained in the Wheeling area. The previous chapter discussed their fifth and sixth cousins, respectively, the six individuals from the fifth generation in the Henry line and the seven individuals from the sixth generation in the Henry line who remained in the Wheeling area.

The ten individuals from the fifth generation of the two lines were born between 1938 and 1982, and the eleven individuals from the sixth generation were born between 1980 and 1994. It is much more difficult to find information on these (mostly) living individuals.

Chapter X concluded that the only potential continuing connection between the two lines of the Serig family based on physical proximity was between descendants of Leah Ries (nee Serig) and descendants of Ilene Mann (nee Schultze), her third cousin once removed. This was based on the slim evidence that Leah lived about a fifteen-minute walk from Ilene in the 1930s. However, Leah, who turned 37 in 1940, was much older than Ilene, who turned nine in 1940.

On the Henry side, Ilene Mann's (nee Schultze) daughter, Linda Mann, and some of Linda's children, Ilene's grandchildren, still live in the Wheeling area. On the Augustus side, only one of Leah Ries' descendants lives in the Wheeling area, her granddaughter, Barbara Sue (Suzie) Palmer (nee Ries), who lives in Dillonvale, Ohio, 18 miles north of Wheeling. However, it is doubtful that Linda is aware that her mother lived near Suzie Palmer's grandmother more than eighty years ago, and that they are in fact related as fifth cousins.

Chapter XIII –
Charles Serig and His Descendants

This chapter is focused on Charles Edward Serig (1923 – 2003), indicated in **bold** in the family tree on the next page, and his descendants. Charles was known by his siblings and earliest friends as "Bus" and by his later friends as "Chuck." Chuck is a member of the fourth generation of the Augustus line.

Chuck Serig was born in Wheeling on November 9, 1923 to Louis Clifford Serig (1900 – 1977) and Loma Sarah Agnes Ward (1901 – 1938), the second of their five sons. Chuck's father, Louis, was the fifth of nine children of Louis August Serig (1871 – 1946) and Amelia Eberling (1874 – 1923). Louis August's mother, Chuck's great-grandmother, was Matilda Serig (1845 – 1992), but his great-grandfather is unknown. Chuck's 2x great-grandfather was Augustus Serig (1812 – 1862) who emigrated from Germany to the Unites States in the late 1830s.

Chuck's mother, Loma Ward, was the third of fourteen children of Charles Augustus Ward (1875 – 1955) and Edna L. Daugherty (1882 – 1955). Charles and Edna were married on July 4, 1899 in Allegheny, Pennsylvania. Their first child, Walter, was born on December 20, 1899. Their second child, William, was born eleven months later in November of 1900, and Loma was born another thirteen months later in December of 1901.

Loma's grandfather was Thomas Ward, who was born in 1846 in East Bethlehem Township, Pennsylvania. He married Sara Stametts about 1865 in Bridgeport, Pennsylvania. Loma's great-grandfather, also Thomas Ward (1811 – 1891), married Elizabeth Williams (1817 – 1846) in 1835. Loma's 2x great-grandfather, Stephen Ward, married Hannah Thurston in Berkeley, West Virginia (then Virginia) in 1799.

Louis and Loma were married in Wheeling on January 24, 1921. Their first child, Louis Albert Serig, was born on June 13, 1922 and died 13 months later on July 13, 1923. Louis Albert is buried in the Greenwood Cemetery.

Chuck was Louis and Loma's second child, born on November 9, 1923, less than four months after his brother's death. Chuck's grandmother, Amelia, died two weeks later on November 24, 1923. She was 49 years old and died of chronic myocarditis (an inflammation of the heart muscle). She is buried in the Greenwood Cemetery in Wheeling.

Augustus Serig Family Tree

Augustus Serig (1812 – 1862) m: Sophia Mary Elizabeth (1813 – 1888) about 1839

- Matilda Serig (1845 – 1892) m: Louis Harding (1840 – 1869)
  - Louis August Serig (1871 – 1946) m: Amelia Eberling (1874 – 1923) in 1893
    - Louis Clifford Serig (1900 – 1977) m: Loma Ward (1901 – 1938) in 1921
      - **Charles Serig** (1923 – 2003) m: Ruth Klinkler (1924 – 2007) in 1945
        - Janet Serig (1947) m: John Nixon (1946) in 1972
          - Jonathan Nixon (1980) m: Alexis Orban (1985) in 2007; d: 2009; m: Morgan Johnson (1989) in 2014
            - Julia Nixon (2005)
            - Arielle Nixon (2007)
          - Jessica Nixon (1982) m: Matthew Kuchera (1984) in 2007; d: 2008; m: Shawn Rine in 2009; d: 2019
            - Isabella Rine (2008)
            - Miley Rine (2011)
            - Jaxson Rine (2013)
        - Karen Serig (1955) m: Ross Jennings (1952) in 1982
          - Chandler Jennings (1992)
        - Kevin Serig (1955) m: Suellyn Vargo (1956) in 1974; d: in 1986; m: Kathy Gitlin (nee Blumling, 1961) in 1988
          - Michael Serig (1978) m: Shelby Barr (1977) in 2003
            - Avery Serig (2007)
            - Brooke Serig (2008)
          - Michelle Serig (1978) m: Jason Wood (1970) in 2000; d: 2014
            - Jake Wood (2000)
          - Stephanie Serig (1979) m: Wayne Diehl (1976) in 2002; d: in 2006
            - Morgan Diehl (1999)
            - Mason Diehl (2003)
          - Amy Serig (1986) m: Joe Moses (1955) in 2013
            - Elijah Moses (2016)

Chuck's younger brother, Jack William, was born on August 3, 1928. Chuck's next brother, Ward, was born on October 2, 1933, and the final brother, Joe, was born on April 18, 1935.

In 1930, the family was living at 4003 Wood Street in Wheeling, and Chuck's father, Louis, was working as a bookkeeper for a fish company. The 1934 city directory shows that sometime after 1930 the family moved about a mile north to 2717 Jacob Street.

Chuck's mother, Loma, died on August 24, 1938, leaving behind four sons, ages 14, 10, 4, and 3. She is buried in the Greenwood Cemetery.

The next year, Chuck's father, Louis, married Mary Alice Coulter (1904 – 1968). In both 1930 and 1934, Mary was living with her mother and two siblings at 3531 Chapline Street, about a half mile north of where Chuck's family was living on Wood Street. In 1930 Mary was 25 years old, single, and working as a sorter in a car factory.

By 1940, the family had moved to 1004 Fourth Street in Portsmouth City, Virginia, and Chuck's father, Louis, was working as a clerk-typist at the Navy yard. Chuck did not get along well with his stepmother, and later that year, on December 10, 1940, at the age of seventeen, he enlisted in the Navy, a full year before Pearl Harbor. Because of his age, he needed his father's permission to enlist. He served in the Navy until October 1945, two months after Japan's unconditional surrender.

During the early part of the war, Chuck was assigned to the USS Albemarle, but for much of the war he was assigned to the USS Yorktown. The original Yorktown was an aircraft carrier that was commissioned in 1937 and was active in the Pacific during the war. This Yorktown was damaged at the Battle of the Coral Sea and then sunk at the Battle of Midway in June 1942. After the original Yorktown was sunk, the Bon Homme Richard, a new carrier that was under construction at the time, was renamed in honor of the Yorktown, and commissioned in April 1943. Chuck spent much of the war assigned to this ship, which was nicknamed the "fighting lady" and was involved in the war in the Pacific until the Japanese surrender.

Chuck's brother, Jack, after retiring from a career in the military (see next chapter), constructed a webpage with stories from those days. One story is about his older brother, Chuck, while he served on the Yorktown. As Jack tells the story, long after the war he was in Charleston, South

Carolina, where the Yorktown was permanently docked as a museum. While touring the ship, he asked one of the volunteer guides, who he refers to below as "the judge" because he had been a lawyer and a magistrate, if he had served on the Yorktown, and if he recalled someone named Charles Serig. The answer was "yes" to both questions. Jack then asked him to talk about the time the Yorktown was hit by a Japanese kamikaze bomb. Here is how Jack described what the guide told him, along with what Chuck had told him over the years.

> When we were back on the hangar deck, I asked "the judge" to show me where the one and only Kamikaze's bomb had penetrated the fleet's air defenses and found its mark. As we proceeded toward a starboard opening extending out beyond the hangar deck, Don stated that of the 109 combat engagements the ship had been in between 1943 and 1945 the single bomb strike was the only time any Japanese plane had been successful in hitting the ship. The attacking plane carrying the bomb had been shot down and crashed in the open sea. However, the bomb found its mark just below and behind the captain's bridge where Don was on duty at the time entering the battle scenes in the ship's log every 15 seconds.
>
> Don explained exactly where the delayed fuse bomb had struck, how it skittered down along the outside metal plating of the ship and finally exploded below the hangar deck into the bunkroom that he, my brother Charles, and ten other quartermaster bunkmates occupied when they rested or were sleeping. Fortunately, it was not occupied at the time. Unfortunately, in areas adjacent to the bunkroom there were 5 KIA (killed in action) and 28 WIA (wounded in action) resulting from the bomb's explosive blast.
>
> At this point in the story is where it becomes personal. My brother, Charles, (family calls him Bus or Buster) was off duty at the time of the sneak attack by the Jap plane. He had decided to leave his bunkroom and go to the flight deck to take a smoke and catch some air. That's where he was when he saw the Kamikaze and watched the bomb it had dropped angling closer and closer toward the Yorktown.
>
> After the explosion the medics found my brother unconscious on the flight deck. Loading him onto a stretcher they raced to the nearest sickbay. Seeing no signs of wounds through his clothing the medics undressed him and found nothing that would clarify his unconscious state. My brother had simply fainted likely from the internal terror he experienced while watching the bomb come c-l-o-s-e-r and c-l-o-s-e-r.

Chuck was discharged from the Navy on October 24, 1945 at the rank of Quartermaster third class. Ten days later, on November 3, 1945, he married Ruth Klinkler in Wheeling.

Ruth's parents were Albert George Klinkler (1895 – 1994) and Katharine Friedhof (1896 – 1961). They were both born in Wheeling, and were married in 1919. They are both buried in the Greenwood Cemetery. Ruth's grandparents on her father's side were George August Klinkler, (1860 – 1942) and Hannah Zimmer (1863 – 1946). Both were born in West Virginia, and they are also buried in the Greenwood Cemetery. Ruth's great-grandfather was William Klinkler (1814 – 1865), who was born in Germany and emigrated to Wheeling at some point.

On her mother's side, Ruth's grandfather was Joseph "Peter" Friedhof (1859 – 1939). He was born in Germany, came to Wheeling in 1872, and married Matilda Kremer (1861 – 1909) in Wheeling in 1892. Matilda's father, Philip Kremer (1824 – 1912), was born in Germany.

In 1930, Ruth was living with her parents and her older brother, Robert, at 2511 26th Street, about a mile from where Louis and his family were living on Wood Street. Ruth's father, Albert, was a cutter in a box factory. However, by 1934 Ruth's family had moved to 2511 Jacob Street, and Chuck's family had moved to 2717 Jacob Street. The two houses were less than a five-minute walk from each other. Albert was a foreman in a box factory, and Robert was a nailer in a box factory.

Two years after they were married, Ruth and Chuck had their first child, Janet, born on November 17, 1947. More than seven years later, on March 30, 1955, Ruth gave birth to twins, Karen and Kevin.

In the early 1950s, the family lived in South Wheeling at 4348 Wood Street, about three blocks from where Chuck had lived as a child. In 1955, they moved to 52 Waddle Avenue in Elm Grove, about five miles east of downtown Wheeling. The construction of Interstate 70 in 1966 caused the family to move down the hill a few blocks toward route 40, to 104 Atkinson Avenue, where they remained for nearly twenty years.

Chuck worked for many years for Wheeling Machine Company, approximately where the Riesbeck grocery store is currently located. Shortly after merging with Joy Manufacturing in 1983, the company moved its Wheeling plant to Visalia, California, and Chuck was one of a handful of employees sent to California to open the new plant. Ruth and Chuck stayed in California for about four years before Chuck retired and they returned to Wheeling.

Chuck was an avid bowler, bowling a 300 game in 1987, and he took up golf later in life. Chuck died on March 7, 2003, and Ruth died on February 6, 2007. They are both buried in the Our Lady of Seven Dolors Cemetery in Triadelphia, West Virginia.

The Children of
Charles Serig (1923 – 2003) and Ruth Klinkler (1924 – 2007)

Janet Ruth Serig (1947) was born on November 17, 1947 in Wheeling. She graduated from Wheeling Central Catholic High School in 1965 and married John Nixon (1946) in 1972. John graduated from Wheeling Central Catholic High School in 1964, and served several years in the military prior to their marriage, including a tour in Vietnam.

On the Nixon side, John's relatives stretch back at least three generations in West Virginia. His great-grandfather was Jerome Nixon (1847 – 1922), married to Salome Brice (1851 – 1936). Both are buried in the Clermont Cemetery in Boothsville, West Virginia, about 70 miles southeast of Wheeling. One of their sons, John Sidney Nixon (1885 – 1977), John's grandfather, is buried in the Greenwood Cemetery in Wheeling. He and his family first appear in the Wheeling area in the 1930 census, when John's father, Harold Nixon (1914 – 1968), was sixteen years old. Harold married Rose Baller (1917 – 1986) in 1940. Rose was born in Italy and came to the United States in 1919 with her parents and two sisters.

Janet and John have two children, Jonathan Harold Nixon (1980) and Jessica Amber Nixon (1982). They are both graduates of Wheeling Park High School, Jonathan in 1998, and Jessica in 2000. They are also both graduates of West Liberty State College (now University), Jonathan in 2002 and Jessica in 2004.

Jonathan married Alexis Orban (1985) in 2007, and they divorced in 2009. They had two children, Julia (2005) and Arielle (2007). Jonathan married Morgan Johnson (1989) in 2014. They reside in the Wheeling area.

Jessica married Matthew Kuchera (1984) in 2007, and they divorced in 2008. She married Shawn Rine (1977) in 2009, and they divorced in 2019. Jessica and Shawn have three children, Isabella (2008), Miley Grace (2011), and Jaxson (2013). Jessica and her children live in Moundsville, about eleven miles south of Wheeling.

Karen Sue Serig (1955) was born on March 30, 1955 in Wheeling. She graduated from Wheeling Central Catholic High School in 1973, and attended Wheeling Jesuit College and West Liberty State College before moving to Houston in the late summer of 1979. In Houston, she took a job at Rice University, where she met her future husband Ross Jennings (1952) in the spring of 1980. Ross was born in San Francisco, and was a third generation San Franciscan on his mother's side. His father's family dates to pre-Revolutionary War days in South Carolina, and over succeeding generations had moved westward, to Kentucky, to Tennessee, to Oregon, to Washington, and then to California. His parents were high school sweethearts at Balboa High School in San Francisco, class of 1939.

Ross' family moved to Sacramento when he was three years old. He graduated from the University of California at Davis in 1974, and had completed an MBA degree at the University of California at Los Angeles in 1979 prior to meeting Karen in Houston.

In the summer of 1981 Karen and Ross drove to Wheeling for Ross to meet Karen's family, and then drove to California where Ross was to begin a doctoral program in business administration. They were married on September 4, 1982, returning to Wheeling for the wedding.

Upon completion of his doctoral program, Ross accepted a position as an assistant professor in accounting at the University of Texas at Austin, where he remained for the next 34 years, retiring in 2020. Shortly after arriving in Austin, Karen completed her bachelor's degree in geography at the University of Texas, taking additional classes to earn a teaching certificate. Karen and Ross currently split their time between their home in Austin, and a second home in Truckee, California, about fifteen miles north of Lake Tahoe.

Karen and Ross have one son, Chandler Philip Jennings (1992). He is a 2014 graduate of Pomona College in Southern California, and currently lives in Denver, Colorado.

Kevin Allen Serig (1955), Karen's twin brother, was born on March 30, 1955 in Wheeling. He graduated from Wheeling Central Catholic High School in 1973, and shortly thereafter began working in the coal mines. Kevin later earned a bachelor's degree in Psychology from West Liberty State College (now University) in 1996, and a master's degree in Social Work from West Virginia University in 1999.

He married Suellyn M. Vargo (1956) in 1974. They were divorced in 1986. Kevin married Kathy Gitlin (nee Blumling, 1961) in 1988.

Kevin and Suellyn had four children, twins Michael Charles (1978) and Michelle Lynn (1978), and daughters Stephanie Marie (1979) and Amy Jo (1985). They are all graduates of Wheeling Park High School, Michael and Michelle in 1996, Stephanie in 1997, and Amy in 2003.

Michael graduated from West Virginia University with a degree in mechanical engineering in 2000. He married Shelby Barr (1977) in 2003. Shelby graduated from West Virginia University with a degree in journalism in 1999 and from the University of Pittsburgh School of Law in 2003. Michael and Shelby have two daughters, Avery Corinne (2007) and Brooke Alexandra (2008). The family lives in Jacksonville, Florida.

Michelle graduated from West Liberty University with a Bachelor of Science in Nursing degree in 2014 and from Franciscan University in 2018 with a Master of Science in Nursing degree and certification as a registered nurse practitioner (CRNP). Michelle married Jason Wood (1970) in 2000. They were divorced in 2014. They have one son, Jake Wood (2000). Michelle lives in Alabama and Jake lives in Wheeling.

Stephanie married Wayne Diehl (1972) in 2002. They were divorced in 2006. They have two children, Morgan Paige Diehl (1999) and Mason Diehl (2003). Stephanie and her two children live in Wheeling.

Amy graduated from West Virginia University with a bachelor's degree in Social Work in 2006 and a master's degree in Social Work in 2008. She married Joseph Moses (1955) in 2013. Amy and Joe have one son, Elijah Joseph (2016). The family lives in Wheeling.

Summary

Fifteen of Charles Serig's descendants continue to live in the Wheeling area, beginning with two of his three children, Janet and Kevin. Janet's two children, Jonathan and Jessica, also continue to live in the Wheeling area, as do Jonathan's two children, Julia and Arielle and Jessica's three children, Isabella, Miley and Jaxson. Two of Kevin's four children, Stephanie and Amy, continue to live in the Wheeling area, as do Stephanie's children, Morgan and Mason, and Amy's son, Elijah. Finally, another of Kevin's grandchildren, Michelle's son Jake, continues to live in the Wheeling area.

Chapter XIV –
Three Serig Brothers and Their Descendants

This chapter is focused on Charles "Chuck" Serig's three younger brothers, Jack (1928 – 2014), Ward (1933 –), and Joe (1935 – 2018). Although the family moved from Wheeling when these three were still children, and they each raised their families elsewhere, Wheeling remained a touchstone for them, and they remained the closest Serig relatives for Chuck and his family.

As with Chuck, his three brothers are members of the fourth generation of the Augustus line of the Serig family. Their father was Louis Clifford Serig (1900 – 1977), their grandfather was Louis August Serig (1871 – 1946), and their great-grandmother was Matilda Serig (1845 – 1992). Their 2x great-grandfather was Augustus Serig (1812 – 1862), who emigrated from Germany to the Unites States in the late 1830s.

Jack William Serig (1928 – 2014)

. . . was born on August 3, 1928 in Wheeling, West Virginia. His family moved to Portsmouth, Virginia in 1939, after his mother died and his father remarried. In August of 1946, according to his World War II draft registration card, Jack was living in Eau Gallie, Florida, about halfway between Miami and Jacksonville. His employer, H.G. Mosley was listed as his next of kin. Jack had stayed on in Eau Gallie to finish high school when his father moved to the Guantanamo Naval Base in Cuba. After graduating he moved to Cuba where he was eventually employed as a paymaster for the base.

After a few years he moved with a friend to Havana where he met and married Lourdes Hernandez (1933 – 2021) in 1950. Lourdes was born in Santiago, Cuba on August 24, 1933, and raised in Havana.

Jack's first career was in the U.S. Army from 1953 to 1972, including international deployments in Germany and Panama, and two tours in Vietnam, in 1962 and again in 1966-67. After his retirement from the military, Jack constructed a webpage with stories from those days. Here is one of the humorous ones.[*]

In 1962, 1 flew Otters for the 18th Aviation Company the length and breadth of Vietnam. There was no armor protecting us except for our issue flak jackets.

There wasn't too much shooting going on as yet and the enemy's aim was particularly poor in the early war stage. But every so often ships landed with bullet holes the crew didn't usually know about until post-flight inspections.

I was able to purloin an extra flak jacket to sit on, thinking that protecting that part of the lower anatomy that lay between the flak vest and me was a high, personal wartime priority.

Fast forward to 1967. There was a lot more shooting going on and the enemy's aim had improved considerably. I was determined, again, with much more reverence than in 1962, to protect "My Boys", as Seinfeld's Cosmo Kramer has humorously called "the family assets."

It wasn't long after my arrival that I "found" the extra flak jacket. Even though the Hueys had much improved armor plating, including the seats, I was determined to provide myself, and my spouse, with the extra protection.

My assignment was flight platoon commander, 281st Assault Helicopter Company. My platoon was split into four detachments, each supporting the Special Forces A camp commanders in each of the four corps.

My job was to hop on Army and Air Force aircraft to get to my split-up crews and provide some flying relief so they could get some rest. I always suggested that my crews purloin extra vests for the very same purpose I have explained, thereby doing my duty to provide the greatest protection I could for my troops. I never surveyed them to determine if what happened to me happened to them.

Now, as you can visualize, sitting on a flak vest in a fixed-wing provides an altogether different effect than sitting on one in a rotary-wing.

In the fixed-wing, your buttocks may slide a little bit back and forth as you decelerate and accelerate. This does not appear to provide any unpleasant problems, as proven by the year I flew the Otter while sitting on a vest. Fixed wing pilots who sat on extra jackets never complained of any problems to my recollection.

However, not so in a Huey helicopter. I flew hour after hour after hour, like so many of you, but I sat on my flak jacket with the knowledge that

---

[*] Jack Serig Stories at: https://www.angelfire.com/fl5/jackserig/

I gave my "Boys" the utmost extra protection that either the Army, or I, could afford.

The problem with sitting on a flak vest in the Huey is that you get a perpendicular movement in relation to your direction of travel and my buttocks wasn't up to withstanding that circular motion, unlike that direct back and forth which the fixed-wing provides.

After many days strapped to Huey cockpits in one corps area or another, the friction from the metal in the vest, against my soft baby-skinned behind, caused, over time, a golf ball-sized boil to eventually form on each cheek, almost perfectly placed one to the other.

I stayed out at the detachments apparently longer than I should have and the boils became abscessed. My butt hurt!

As soon as I got back to Nha Trang, I went immediately to the 5th Special Forces Group surgeon. Now this is when I got hit.

He "shot" the surrounding area of each wound with a needle full of local anesthetic and, when that took effect, he lanced the affected areas. He grounded me for two weeks and issued me a regulation doughnut pillow for my seating comfort.

To this day, 32 years later, I still carry a rounded wound on each buttock. They look like repaired bullet holes' entry markings.

In summary, I have two wounds that occurred while I was in combat or combat support mode flying Hueys in support of the war effort. Even though, so they tell me, I'm not entitled to a Purple Heart, I can show my grandkids where I was "wounded" during the war.

In 1972, while stationed in Panama, Jack retired with the rank of Lt. Colonel. Upon his retirement, he drove the family north on the Panamanian Highway for several months before finally settling in Miami.

Jack's second career was with the Miami-Dade County Public School System as the Director of Safety and Transportation Departments. Jack died on October 17, 2014, and is buried in the South Florida National Cemetery in Lake Worth, Florida.

Jack and Lourdes had five children, Arthur Lewis (1954), Jack William Jr. (1959), Charles Edward (1960), Shawna (1964), Kendrick Allen (1966), all fifth-generation descendants of Augustus Serig.

The Children of
Jack Serig (1928 – 2014) and Lourdes Hernandez (1933 – 2021)

Arthur Louis Serig (1954 –) was born on February 4, 1954 in Havana, Cuba. He married Jan Ellen Kurtz (1952) in Miami in 1976, and they had two children, Shannon (1981) and Shawn (1984), both born in Miami. Arthur and Jan divorced in 1993. Arthur married Rene Wagner (1960) in 1995, and they divorced in 1999. Arthur later married Jeanette Diadone (1952). Arthur and Jeanette currently live in Boca Raton, Florida.

The Jack Serig Family Tree

Augustus Serig (1812 – 1862) m: Sophia Mary Elizabeth (1813 – 1888) about 1839

- Matilda Serig (1845 – 1892) m: Louis Harding (1840 – 1869)
  - Louis August Serig (1871 – 1946) m: Amelia Eberling (1874 – 1923) in 1893
    - Louis Clifford Serig (1900 – 1977) m: Loma Ward (1901 – 1938) in 1921
      - **Jack Serig** (1928) m: Lourdes Hernandez (1933 – 2021) in 1950
        - Arthur Lewis Serig (1954) m: Jan Ellen Kurtz (1952) in 1976; d: in 1993; m: Rene Wagner (1960) in 1995; d: in 1999; m: Jeanette Diadone (1952)
          - Shannon Serig (1981)
          - Shawn Serig (1984)
        - Jack William Serig, Jr. (1959 – 2011)
        - Charles Edward Serig (1960) m: Maria del Carmen Padron (1963) in 1987
          - Christian Alexander (1992)
          - Lauren Nichole (1994)
        - Shawna Serig (1964) m: Julio Daniel Larosa in 1991; d: in 1993; m: Mark Lucas; m: Mark William Kelsch in 2000
        - Kendrick Allen Serig (1966) m: Margaret Mary Binder in 1998

Jack William Serig, Jr. (1959 – 2011) was born on November 1, 1959 in Miami. Jack Jr. had Down Syndrome. He died on November 17, 2011, at the age of 52, and is buried in the Woodlawn Park Cemetery South in Miami.

Charles Edward Serig (1960 –) was born on December 4, 1960 at Ft. Riley, Kansas. He married Maria del Carmen Padron (1963) in 1987. They have two children, Christian Alexander (1992) and Lauren Nichole (1994). Charles currently lives in Miami Lakes, Florida.

Shawna Lee Serig (1964 –) was born on June 23, 1964 at Ft. Carson, Colorado. She married Julio Daniel Larosa in 1991. They divorced in 1993. She may have also married Mark Lucas. She married Mark William Kelsch in 2000 in Broward, Florida. They live in Indialantic, Florida, about halfway between Miami and Jacksonville.

Kendrick Allen Serig (1966 –) was born on June 23, 1966 in Stuttgart, Germany. He married Margaret Mary Binder in Miami in 1998. They may be divorced. Ken currently lives in Miami.

Ward Earl Kendrick Serig (1933 –)

. . . was born on October 2, 1933 in Wheeling, West Virginia. His mother died in August of 1938, when he was four years old. His father remarried the next year, and the family moved to Portsmouth City, Virginia. Ward attended Mooseheart Child City and School, about 38 miles west of Chicago, while his father was stationed at Guantanamo Naval Base. Ward married Donnie Smith (1933 –) in 1955. Ward and Donnie currently live in Pensacola, Florida.

Ward enlisted in the Navy in 1953 as a Naval Aviation Cadet in Pensacola. About that time, a couple he knew through the Reorganized Church of Jesus Christ of the Latter Day Saints (RLDS) arranged for him to go to a church dance with a friend of theirs, Donnie Smith. Donnie picked Ward up in front of a downtown hotel, they went to dinner and the dance with the other couple, and the rest, as they say, is history.

Ward served twenty-three-and-a-half years in the Navy, primarily as a helicopter pilot and flight instructor. His initial assignments were in San Diego and Pensacola. In 1959, he resigned from active duty to return to college, earning a degree in mathematics in Tallahassee, Florida. Two years later he reactivated, and had various assignments in San Diego, Norfolk, Pensacola, Vietnam, and Puerto Rico.

His tour in Vietnam was from April 1969 to April 1970. He was Officer-in-Charge of a four plane detachment for four months, and Training and Assistant Operations Officer at squadron headquarters for eight months.

After his assignment to Puerto Rico, Ward returned to Pensacola for his last three years. He retired from the Navy on June 1, 1982. For the next 25 years he was employed by a contractor as an instrument flight instructor at NAS Whiting in Pensacola.

While on tour in Vietnam in July, 1969, an article in the *Beckley Post-Herald* included the following:

> After joining a river patrol unit for half the day, the news tour made its way to the Seawolves' headquarters. When introduced to the unit's commanding officer. Commander Ward Serig, the handsome Navy officer in his beret (see pictures) remarked that he hailed originally from Wheeling. His is the brother of Charles Serig of Elm Grove, a Wheeling suburb, and still considers Wheeling his hometown though long Navy service has kept him living in other locales around the world for most of his life now.

The picture referred to in the article had the following caption:

> Comdr. Ward Serig, former Wheeling man and brother of Charles Serig of Elm Grove is seen here with Post-Herald editor E. J. Hodel and his unit's unofficial mascot, a Vietnamese-type dog which is called "Just Dog," standing before the Seawolves dragon insignia. Serig's men fly "Huey" helicopter gunships. The 'copters carry powerful rockets and machineguns which give them a "big sting" against the guerillas of the Communists in the Vietnam delta country.

Ward was also active in the Reorganized Church of Jesus Christ of the Latter Day Saints (RLDS).[*] He and his three brothers were all baptized into the church when they were about eight years old. However, only Ward and his younger brother, Joe, were active in the church throughout their adult lives. As an adult, his oldest brother, Charles ("Chuck"), became a Catholic, and his next oldest brother, Jack, married a Catholic and though he remained a member in the RLDS, he was no longer active.

As early as the mid 1950s Ward and Donnie served as youth leaders in Pensacola, and Ward directed a camp for high school students for three summers. Ward was also ordained as an elder while they were in Pensacola. While on leave from the Navy in Tallahassee, Ward took his turn preaching at the local congregation.

At each of his postings in San Diego, Norfolk, and Pensacola, Ward served in various capacities for the church, as a youth leader, teaching

---

[*] In 2001, the Reorganized Church of Jesus Christ of the Latter Day Saints was renamed as the Community of Christ.

Sunday school, preaching on Sunday, and so forth. After his tour in Vietnam, Ward spent five years in Pensacola during which he served for two years as District President, responsible for ten or eleven congregations.

After returning to Pensacola from Puerto Rico, Ward served as pastor of the Milton, Florida congregation for two years, and again as District President for another two years. In 1997 he was ordained an evangelist. According to the Community of Christ website,

> Evangelists are ordained to be ministers of blessing, witnessing of Jesus Christ and responsive to the reconciling and redeeming influence of the Holy Spirit in the lives of persons, serving in multiple ministries according to the unique gifts and callings of each evangelist.

Ward and Donnie have four children, Steven Allen (1957), Joy Loma (1958), Kendrick Earl (1963), and Julie Elizabeth (1969) and numerous grandchildren and great-grandchildren, as summarized in the family tree on the following page.

The Children of
Ward Serig (1933 –) and Donnie Smith (1933 –)

Steven Allen Serig (1957 –) was born on February 5, 1957. Steven married Melinda Gail McMillan (1964) in 1987, and they divorced in 1988. In 1989, Steven married Donna Joan Guiasola (1956), and they divorced in 1990. In 2010, Steven married Kathleen Evans (1955). Steven and his first wife, Melinda, had three children, Tyanna (1981), Nathaniel (1983), and Crystal Anne (1985).

Tyanna married James Fuller, Jr. (1980), and they have two children, James Fuller, III (2003), and Michael Fuller (2005).

Nathaniel married Elizabeth (?) and they have four children, Noah (2013), Faith (2016), Naomi (2017, and Torianna (2020).

Crystal Anne married Josh Jones (?) in 2003, and they have two children, Micah (2011) and Olivia Grace (2014). Crystal has one more child, Colin Hargar (2018), but the parents are now separated.

Joy Loma Serig (1958 –) was born on November 30, 1958. Joy married Charles Wilson in 1979, and they divorced in 1993. They had one child, Jill (1982). Jill also has one child, Jaxson Favreau (2009) with partner, James Favreau.

The Ward Serig Family Tree

Augustus Serig (1812 – 1862) m: Sophia Mary Elizabeth (1813 – 1888) about 1839

- Matilda Serig (1845 – 1892) m: Louis Harding (1840 – 1869)
  - Louis August Serig (1871 – 1946) m: Amelia Eberling (1874 – 1923) in 1893
    - Louis Clifford Serig (1900 – 1977) m: Loma Ward (1901 – 1938) in 1921
      - **Ward Serig** (1933 –) m: Donnie M. Smith (1933 –) in 1955
        - Steven Allen Serig (1957) m: Melinda McMillan (1964) in 1987; d: in 1988; m: Kathleen Evans (1955) in 2010
          - Tyanna Serig (1981) (mother is Melinda) m: James Fuller Jr. (1980)
            - James Fuller III (2003)
            - Michael Fuller (2005)
          - Nathaniel Serig (1983) (mother is Melinda) m: Elizabeth
            - Noah Serig (2013)
            - Faith Serig (2016)
            - Naomi Serig (2017)
            - Torianna Serig (2020)
          - Crystal Anne Serig (1983) (mother is Melinda) m: Josh Jones (1982) in 2003,
            - Micah Jones (2011)
            - Olivia Grace Jones (2014)
            - Colin Harger (2018) (father is Harger, now separated)
        - Joy Loma Serig (1958) m: Charles Wilson (1958) in 1979, d: in 1993
          - Jill Wilson (1982)
            - Jaxson Favreau (2009) (father is James Favreau)
        - Kendrick Allen Serig (1963) m: Lorrie Scrivner (1966) in 1995
          - Avi Joshua Serig (1999) m: Madelyn Ward (2001) in 2020.
          - Kira Serig (2004)
          - Asa Trustin Serig (2007)
        - Julie Elizabeth Serig (1969) m: Howard Steele (1968) in 1995; m: Clifford Ellis Mayo (1969) in 2004
          - Lauren Serig (1988) (father is Joey Von Axelson) m: Matthew Jarrett (1988) in 2006.
            - Abby Lynn Jarrett (2005)
            - Finley Mae Jarrett (2019)
          - Hannah Steele (1996) (parents divorced)
          - Carly Mayo (2009)

Kendrick Earle Serig (1963 –) was born on August 28, 1963. Ken married Lorrie Scrivner (1966) in 1995. They have one son, Avi Joshua (1999). Avi married Madelyn Ward (2001) and they have two children, Kira (2004) and Asa Trustin (2007). Ken and Lorrie live in Lees Summit, Missouri.

Julie Elizabeth Serig (1969 –) was born on August 27, 1969. Julie married Howard J. E. N. Steele (1968) in 1995. I cannot find a record of their divorce. In 2004, Julie married Clifford Ellis Mayo (1969). They have one daughter, Carly Mayo (2009). Julie also has one child with Joey Von Axelson, Lauren Serig (1988). Lauren married Matthew Jarrett (1988) in 2006, and they have two children, Abby Lynn (2005) and Finley Mae (2019).

Joe Allen Serig (1935 – 2018)

. . . was born on April 18, 1935 in Wheeling, West Virginia. His mother died in August of 1938, when he was three years old. His father remarried the next year, and the family moved to Portsmouth City, Virginia. Joe attended Mooseheart Child City and School, about 38 miles west of Chicago, for his middle and high school years while his father was stationed at Guantanamo Naval Base in Cuba.

In 1953-4 Joe was a freshman at Graceland College in Lamoni, Iowa, a private college affiliated with the Reorganized Church of Jesus Christ of Latter Day Saints (RLDS). It was at Graceland College that he met his future wife, Beverly Wilson (1934 –). Beverly's roommate invited her to come live with her in San Jose and go to school there. So, Joe decided he might as well go to San Jose State also.

Joe and Beverly were married on December 27, 1955 in Independence, Missouri. The marriage license lists Joe as a resident of Santa Clara County, California, and Beverly as a resident of Jackson County, Missouri. Joe required his father's assent because he was under the age of 21. Beverly did not require her parent's assent because she was over the age of eighteen.

Joe and Beverly both completed their college degrees in education in San Jose California. Afterwards, Joe taught junior high there and later became a junior high school principal.

Joe began his long career with the RLDS by accepting church employment shortly after finishing college. He was ordained as an elder in 1953, and while in San Jose he served as the pastor for the local congregation.

The family moved to Independence, Missouri in 1971 when Joe became an Appointee for the church in the Christian Education Department. He received his Ph.D. in higher education from the University of Missouri at Kansas City in the mid-70s. Joe was ordained an Apostle in the RLDS in 1982 and served the California, Native American, Europe and Africa regions for 20 years. The RLDS (now Community of Christ) website describes the role of Apostles as follows:

> Members of the Council of Twelve Apostles are high priests called and ordained to be special missionary witnesses. Assigned by the First Presidency, they carry major responsibility for church expansion, and serve as administrative supervisors of field jurisdictions.

Joe died on October 6, 2018, in Independence Missouri, at the age of 83.

Joe and Beverly had four children, Deborah Joan (1958), Marjorie Ellen (1960), Craig Bernard (1962), and Daniel Allen (1969), as well as numerous grandchildren and great-grandchildren, as summarized in the family tree below. Their children were all born in Santa Clara County, California, and they all attended Truman High School in Independence, Missouri after the family moved there.

<h2 style="text-align:center">The Children of
Joe Serig (1935 – 2018) and Beverly Wilson (1934 –)</h2>

Deborah Joan Serig (1958 –) was born on May 18, 1958. Deborah married Marvin Brian Lalone (1957) on June 18, 1977. Deborah and Marvin moved to Michigan in the late 1980s or early 1990s, and they still live there. They have two children, Marvin Floyd (1980) and Katie Jo (1982).

Marvin married Robyn Sue Maurer (1981) in 2004 when both were serving in the Coast Guard. The couple lives in Michigan and they have three children, Lucy Sue (2006), Ty Joseph (2009), and Jack Brian (2010).

Katie married Kendall Robert Leyder (1976) in 2004. The couple lives in Michigan and they have two children, Madelin Marie (2006) and Eben Timothy (2010).

The Joe Serig Family Tree

Augustus Serig (1812 – 1862) m: Sophia Mary Elizabeth (1813 – 1888) about 1839

- Matilda Serig (1845 – 1892) m: Louis Harding (1840 – 1869)
  - Louis August Serig (1871 – 1946) m: Amelia Eberling (1874 – 1923) in 1893
    - Louis Clifford Serig (1900 – 1977) m: Loma Ward (1901 – 1938) in 1921
      - **Joe Allen Serig** (1935 – 2018) m: Beverly Wilson (1934 –) in 1955
        - Deborah Joan Serig (1958) m: Marvin Brian LaLone (1957) in 1977
          - Marvin Floyd LaLone (1980) m: Robyn Maurer (1981) in 2004
            - Lucy Sue LaLone (2006)
            - Ty Joseph LaLone (2009)
            - Jack Brian LaLone (2010)
        - Marjorie Ellen Serig (1960) m: Bobby Ray Mims (1957) in 1982; d: in 2002
          - Kirsten Danielle Mims (1960)
            - Joy Aten Gaither (2019) (father Jared Dwight Gaither)
          - Adrian Drake Mims (1990) m: Tylara Hollowell (1993) in 2017
            - Harlow Lillian Mims (2012)
        - Craig Bernard Serig (1962) m: Lisa Mann (1968) in 2009
          - Jessica Lauren Serig (1986) (mother is Deanna Snider Thomas) m: Steven Owen Murphy (1988) in 2016
            - Wyatt Owen Murphy (2019)
          - Miles Dennis Serig (1993) (mother is Richelle Harris)
        - Daniel Allen Serig (1969) m: Angela Suarez (1972) in 1994
          - Sofia Isabelle Serig (2003)
          - Alexa Marie Serig (2006)

Marjorie Ellen Serig (1960 –) was born on August 29, 1960. Marjorie married Bobby Ray Mims (1957) in 1982, and they divorced in 2002. Marjorie currently lives in Independence, Missouri. Marjorie and Bobby Ray have two children, Kirsten Danielle (1987) and Adrian Drake (1990).

Kirsten's daughter, Joy Aten Gaither, was born on June 10, 2019. Joy's father is Jared Dwight Gaither. Kirsten lives in Denver, Colorado.

Adrian Drake married Tylara Jean Hollowell (1983) in 2017. They have a daughter, Harlow Lillian (2012), and live in Independence, Missouri.

Craig Bernard Serig (1962 –) was born on February 10, 1962. Craig married Deanna Lynn Snider in 1984. Craig also married Richelle Harris, not sure when, probably in early 1990s. Craig married Lisa Mann (1968) in 1999 in Independence Missouri. They currently live in Lees Summit, Missouri.

Craig and his first wife, Deanna, have a daughter, Jessica Lauren (1986). Jessica married Steven Owen Murphy (1988) in 2016. They have a son, Wyatt Owen (2019). Craig and his second wife, Richelle, have a son, Miles Dennis (1993).

Daniel Allen Serig (1969 –) was born on November 1, 1969. Daniel married Angela Suarez (1972) in 1994 in Independence, Missouri. They have two daughters, Sofia (2003) and Alexa (2006), and they live in Massachusetts.

Chapter XV
Summary – The Serig Family in Wheeling

The Henry Line

Henry E. Serig arrived in Wheeling from Germany in the 1830s. As discussed in Chapter II, he had five children, the first American-born generation of the Serig family from the Henry line. Three of those children, Henry J., Louis, and Albert, gave Henry twenty-seven grandchildren, the second generation of the Henry line. Only descendants of Louis and Albert still live in the Wheeling area. Those descendants still living in the Wheeling area are in **bold** in the family tree and discussion below, and are summarized in the table at the end of this chapter.

Three members of the <u>fourth generation</u> of the Henry line still live in the Wheeling area. **Patricia Katherine McKeen** (nee Serig) lives with her husband, Warren McKeen, in Bethany, West Virginia. **Joseph M. McMullen** lives in Moundsville, West Virginia, and **Sally Habig** (nee Muldoon) lives in St. Clairsville, Ohio. Each of these locations is less than thirty miles from the other two. Patricia turns 85 in 2021, and Warren will turn 86. Joseph will be 81 years old in 2021, and Sally will be 71. Patricia and Joseph are first cousins, and likely know each other. Sally is a third cousin to both, so they may not be aware of the connection.

Five members of the <u>fifth generation</u> of the Henry line still live in the Wheeling area. **Dean Serig** lives in Dillonvale, Ohio. **Joseph M. McMullen** lives in Moundsville. **Linda Kaminski** (nee Mann) lives in Wheeling. **Ronald Habig** also lives in Wheeling, and his brother, **Brian Habig** lives in Bridgeport, Ohio. Dillonvale is about thirty miles north of Moundsville, and Wheeling and Bridgeport are in between. In 2021, Dean will be 62, Joseph will be 54, and Linda will be 66. Also in 2021, Ronald will be 42, and Brian will be 39. Dean and Joseph are third cousins, and both are fourth cousins to Linda. Siblings Ronald and Brian are third cousins to Linda, and fourth cousins to Dean and Joseph. Given, the distance of these relations, none of these individuals other than the Habig brothers may be aware of these connections.

Henry Serig Family Tree

Henry Serig (1809 – 1851) m: Mary Christina Dipple (1813 – 1888)

- Louis August Serig (1843 – 1923) m: Sarah Ann Lewellen (1848 – 1927)
  - George August Serig (1871 – 1956) m: Maud Cotts (1877 – 1923)
    - Charles L. Serig (1901 – 1981) married Wilma King ((1900 – 1983)
      - James Louis Serig (1929 – 1992) m: Bonnie Jewell (1925 – 2014)
        - **Dean Serig** (1959, 5th) m: Maria Frankovich (1965) – Dillonvale, Ohio, about 20 miles north of Wheeling
          - **Robert Serig** (1987, 6th) – Dillonvale, Ohio
  - Harry Newton Serig (1883 – 1954) m: Mary Lynch (1888 – 1947)
    - Harold Serig (1909 – 1952) m: Gertrude Foran Bartollas (1909 – 1982)
      - **Patricia Catherine Serig** (1936, 4th) m: Warren McKeen (1934) – Bethany, West Virginia
    - Anna C. Serig (1911 – 1985) m: John McMullen (1897 – 1968) in 1938
      - **Joseph N. McMullen** (1940, 4th) m: Carol Buzas (1941 – 2003) in 1961 – Moundsville
        - **Joseph M. McMullen** (1967, 5th) m: Susan Black (1966 –) – Moundsville
- Albert Serig Sr. (1845 – 1921) m: Sarah Virginia Sykes (1849 – 1944)
  - Sara Serig (1878 – 1970) m: August Schultze (1877 – 1924)
    - William Schultze (1903 – 1979) m: Emma King (1908 – 1994)
      - Ilene Schultze (1931 – 2003) m: Wallace Harry Mann (1931 – 2008)
        - **Linda Mann** (1956, 5th) m: Mark Kaminski (1958) – Wheeling
          - **Kerrie Kaminski** (1992, 6th) – Wheeling
          - **Markie Kaminski** (1993, 6th) – St. Clairsville, Ohio
        - Thomas Mann (1963 – 2005, 5th) m: Teresa Riggs (1959)
          - **Jessica Mann** (1986, 6th) – Wheeling
          - **Morgan Mann** (1992, 6th) – Wheeling
          - **Lindsey Mann** (1994, 6th) – St. Clairsville
  - Albert Serig Jr. (1880 – 1965) m: Anna Mary Schultze (1880 – 1968)
    - Mary K. Serig (1914 – 2009) m: Robert Muldoon (1916 – 1996)
      - **Sally Muldoon** (1950, 4th) m: Roland Habig (1951 –) – St. Clairsville, Ohio
        - **Ronald Habig** (1979, 5th) m: Fallon Kendra Namack (1980) – Wheeling
        - **Brian Habig** (1982, 5th) m: Elizabeth Connell (1980), divorced – Bridgeport, Ohio

Six members of the <u>sixth generation</u> of the Henry line still live in the Wheeling area. **Robert Serig** lives in Dillonvale, Ohio. Sisters **Kerrie Kaminski** lives in Wheeling and **Markie Kaminski** lives in St. Clairsville, Ohio. **Jessica Mann** and **Morgan Mann** live in Wheeling and **Lindsey Mann** lives in St. Clairsville. Dillonvale is about eighteen miles north of Wheeling, and St. Clairsville is about eleven miles west of Wheeling. In 2021, Robert will be 34, Kerrie will be 29, and her sister, Markie, will be 28. Jessica will be 35, her sister, Morgan, will be 29, and her other sister, Lindsey, will be 27. The Kaminksi sisters are first cousins to the Mann sisters, and both sets of sisters are fifth cousins to Robert. Given the distance of the relation between Robert and the two sets of sisters, none of them may be aware of the connection.

The Augustus Line

Augustus Serig (1812 – 1862) and Sophia Mary Elizabeth (known as Elizabeth, last name not known, 1813 – 1888) emigrated from Germany in the 1830s, probably separately, and were married in about 1839. As discussed in Chapter II, they had five children, the first American-born generation of the Serig family from the Augustus line.

Only one of those children, Matilda (1845 – 1892), has descendants who still live in the Wheeling area. Those descendants are members of the fifth, sixth, and seventh American-born generations of the Augustus line. They are in **bold** in the family tree and discussion below, and are summarized in the table at the end of this chapter where they are integrated with descendants of the Henry line in rough physical relation to each other.

Four members of the <u>fifth generation</u> of the Augustus line still live in the Wheeling area, **Marjorie Lofton** (nee Glitsch), who lives in Bridgeport, Ohio, **Janet Nixon**, (nee Serig) and her brother **Kevin Serig**, who both live in Wheeling, and **Barbara Sue "Suzie" Palmer** (nee Ries) who lives in Dillonvale, Ohio. Dillonvale is about eighteen miles north of Wheeling and Bridgeport is across the river from Wheeling. In 2021, Marjorie will turn 83, Janet will turn 74, Kevin will turn 66, and Barbara will turn 59. Siblings Janet and Kevin are second cousins to Suzie, and all three are fourth cousins to Marjorie. Janet and Kevin knew Suzie to some extent as children, but neither is aware of Marjorie or their relation to her.

Augustus Serig Family Tree

Augustus Serig (1812 – 1862) m: Sophia Mary Elizabeth (1813 – 1888) about 1839

- Matilda Serig (1845 – 1892) m: Louis Harding (1840 – 1869)
  - Elizabeth Serig (1864 – 1943) m: John Louis Moore (1863 – 1933) in 1888
    - Carrie Moore (1891 – 1981) m: Ralph Woods (1890 -1955) in 1912
      - Henrietta Woods (1913 – 1991) m: Carl Glitsch (1912 – 1979) in 1934
        - **Marjorie Glitsch** (1938), 5th) m: Gerald Lofton – Bridgeport, Ohio
  - Louis August Serig (1871 – 1946) m: Amelia Eberling (1874 – 1923) in 1893
    - Louis Clifford Serig (1900 – 1977) m: Loma Ward (1901 – 1938) in 1921
      - Charles Serig (1923 – 2003) m: Ruth Klinkler (1924 – 2007) in 1945
        - **Janet Serig** (1947, 5th) m: John Nixon in 1972 – Wheeling
          - **Jonathan Nixon** (1980, 6th) m: Alexis Orban (1985) in 2007; d: 2009; – Yorkville, Ohio
            - **Julia Nixon** (2005, 7th) Rayland, Ohio ten miles north of Wheeling on the Ohio side of the river. 2.5 miles north of Yorkville.
            - **Arielle Nixon** (2007, 7th) Rayland, Ohio
          - **Jessica Nixon** (1982, 6th) m: Matthew Kuchera (1984) in 2007; d: 2008; m: Shawn Rine in 2009; d: 2019 – Moundsville
            - **Isabella Rine** (2008, 7th) – Moundsville
            - **Miley Rine** (2011, 7th) – Moundsville
            - **Jaxson Rine** (2013, 7th) – Moundsville
        - **Kevin Serig** (1955, 5th) m: Sue Vargo in 1974; d: in 1986; m: Kathy Gitlin (1961, nee Blumling) in 1988 – Wheeling
          - Michelle Serig (1978) m: Jason Wood (1970) in 2000; d: 2014
            - **Jake Wood** (2000, 7th) – Wheeling
          - **Stephanie Serig** (1979, 6th) m: Wayne Diehl (1976) in 2002; d: in 2006 – Wheeling
            - **Morgan Diehl** (1999, 7th) – Wheeling
            - **Mason Diehl** (2003, 7th) – Wheeling
          - **Amy Serig** (1986, 6th) m: Joe Moses (1955) in 2013 – Wheeling
            - **Elijah Moses** (2016, 7th) – Wheeling
    - Leah A Serig (1902 – 1995) m: George Ries (1896 – 1974) in 1921
      - George Ries (1925 – 1987) m: Mary Burger (1931 – 2017) in 1955
        - **Barbara ("Suzie") Ries** (1962, 5th) m: James Paknik in 1978, d: in 1980, m: James Palmer in 1982, d: in 1991 – Dillonvale, Ohio

Four members of the <u>sixth generation</u> of the Augustus line still live in the Wheeling area, **Jonathan Nixon** lives in Yorkville, Ohio, his sister, **Jessica Rine** (nee Nixon), lives in Moundsville, and **Stephanie Serig** and her sister **Amy Moses** (nee Serig) both live in Wheeling. Yorkville is about nine miles north of Wheeling and Moundsville is about eleven miles south of Wheeling. In 2021, Jonathan will turn 41, Jessica will turn 39, Stephanie will turn 42, and Amy will turn 35. Siblings Jonathan and Jessica are first cousins to siblings Stephanie and Amy, and all are well-known to each other.

Nine members of the <u>seventh generation</u> of the Augustus line still live in the Wheeling area. Sisters **Julia** and **Arielle Nixon**, live in Rayland, Ohio, 10 miles north of Wheeling. Siblings **Isabella**, **Miley**, and **Jaxson Rine**, live in Moundsville, eleven miles south of Wheeling. Siblings **Morgan** and **Mason Diehl**, and first cousins **Jake Wood** and **Eli Moses** all live in Wheeling. In 2021, Julia will turn 16, Arielle will turn 14, Isabella will turn 13, Miley will turn 10, Jaxson will turn 8, Morgan will turn 22, Mason will turn 18, Jake will turn 21, and Eli will turn 5.

The Rine siblings are second cousins to both Jake and Eli, and their parents are well-known to each other. The Nixon siblings live with their mother who is not in contact with the Serigs, and the two girls are not well-known by either their first cousins, the Rine siblings, or their second cousins, Jake and Eli.

The Henry and Augustus Lines

This project began as a search for how the descendants of two immigrant brothers who came to Wheeling almost two hundred years ago could live in the same city without being aware of their relation to each other. By 1850, the older brother, Henry, was operating a grocery store, and his younger brother, Augustus, was working as a laborer, an indication of a division in their economic status. When Henry died in 1851, his youngest son, Albert, was only six years old, the same age as Augustus' daughter, Matilda. His death may have reduced the interaction between the two families while some of the children were still quite young.

Henry's brother, Augustus, died in 1862, when his daughter, Matilda, was seventeen. She became pregnant a year later, out of wedlock, and gave birth in August of 1864. Her unconventional life thereafter may have inhibited contact with her cousins, Louis and Albert, at this early date.

By the turn of the century, both families were scattered around the Wheeling area, not only in Wheeling itself, but to the east in Triadelphia, to the south in Marshall County, and across the river in Ohio. However, there were two locations in Wheeling where there were possible connections between members of the two lines of the Serig family based on physical proximity, on Wheeling Island and in South Wheeling.

However, these possible connections were tenuous indeed, depending on the fact that Leah Ries (nee Serig) had lived about a fifteen-minute walk from Ilene Mann (nee Schultze) more than eighty years ago, and on whether descendants of Leah knew descendants of Ilene, her third cousin once removed. As a further impediment, Leah was much older than Ilene. Leah turned 37 in 1940 and Ilene was only turning nine.

I found only one of Leah Ries' descendants who still lives in the Wheeling area, her granddaughter Barbara Sue "Suzie" Palmer (nee Ries), who lives in Dillonvale, Ohio, 18 miles north of Wheeling. On the Henry side, Ilene Mann's (nee Schultze) daughter, Linda Mann, and some of Linda's children, Ilene's grandchildren, still live in the Wheeling area. However, I doubt they are aware of each other and that they are in fact related as fifth cousins.

However, Serigs from the two lines of the family do occasionally cross paths. For example, Amy, who inspired this project with her visit to Greenwood Cemetery, told me that she often crossed paths with Brian Habig at West Virginia University where they had common friends, not realizing they were fifth cousins once removed.

Two other accidental contacts occurred at Wheeling Hospital where Maria Serig (nee Frankovich), Dean Serig's wife, works. On separate occasions, Kevin Serig and his sister, Janet Nixon (nee Serig), went to the hospital and encountered Maria and saw her name tag with her last name as Serig. Maria told Janet that she thought Kevin's voice sounded much like her husband's, making her wonder at the time if they were related. They are fifth cousins.

Finally, Albert Serig Jr.'s son, John "Jack" Serig (1917 – 2004) is important to this story even though he did not have children. In the latter half of the twentieth century, he was the most visible Serig from the Henry line in Wheeling, and the person my father-in-law, Chuck Serig, referred to as the "other" Serig who was no relation.

According to Jack's obituary he . . .

. . . was a retired salesman and supervisor from Wheeling Electric Company for 40 years; a retired Realtor from the George W. Petroplus firm, a retired Chairman of the Board for 28 years for the Wheeling Housing Authority. He was a 50 year member and Past Master of Ohio Lodge #1 A.F. & A. M.; past High Priest, Wheeling Union Chapter #1; a 32 degree Scottish Rite Mason; member of the Osiris Shrine, Royal Order of Jesters; past commander of the Shrine Legion of Honor; past Director of the YMCA; charter member of the Jr. Chamber of Commerce; past member of the Wheeling Elks Lodge BPOE #28; past Director and member of the Wheeling Country Club; past treasurer of the Big Band 200 Club; past member of the Board of Director of Altenheim; social member of Jupiter Tequesta Methodist Church, and a former Director for Progressive Bank in Wheeling. In addition to his parents, he was preceded in death by his first wife, Mary T. Yeager Serig. Surviving are his wife Rose Lee Crago Serig; a sister, Kathleen Muldoon of Wheeling, a niece, Sally Habig and her husband, Ron of Wheeling, a nephew Robert Muldoon of Wheeling; two grandnephews Ronald and Brain Habig of Wheeling and a host of special friends. . . Internment in Greenwood Cemetery, Wheeling.

The one place where he and Chuck may have interacted was at the Elks Lodge where both were members. If they met there, they may have scratched their heads and wondered how two people with the same unusual last name could live in the same small town and not be related. They probably couldn't trace their ancestors far enough back to realize that they were in fact third cousins, once removed. I can imagine a conversation like this.

"Is your last name Serig?"

"That's right, I'm Chuck Serig."

"The boys over there told me you were a Serig, I'm Jack Serig."

"Small world."

"Think there's any chance we're related?"

"I don't think so, I know all the Serigs I'm related to."

"Who was your father?"

"Louis, Louis Clifford Serig. My grandfather was a Louis too, Louis August Serig. Know them?"

"No, my father was Albert Serig and his father was Albert Serig too."

"Never heard of them."

"Just a coincidence I guess."

"Yea, I guess so."

Distant cousins do not remain in contact by accident or without some effort. One example in Wheeling of a family that has stayed connected is John Nixon's. John's mother was one of six siblings and together they had many children, John's first cousins, many of whom remained in Wheeling. Those children of course had children of their own, for example, Jonathan and Jessica, second cousins to the children of John's first cousins. The second cousins are now old enough to have their own children, like the Rine siblings, John's grandchildren and third cousins to the grandchildren John's first cousins. Each year the extended family gathers to stuff sausages the old Italian way. For many, this is an important event that they hope to convey to the fourth cousins and beyond. But doing so takes effort, it requires that someone organize and host the event.

Maintaining such connections is certainly not guaranteed, even for families with unusual last names living in the same small town. In the case of the Serigs in Wheeling, it appears that the two lines of the family just drifted apart over time. Maybe the two immigrant brothers were just not that close to each other in the first place. Maybe a succeeding generation lacked a critical person to take charge of keeping the family connected. Maybe within each generation the age differences were too great, or the economic differences were too great, to share common life experiences on which to base a connection. Maybe too many of the families chose to leave the area.

The descendants of Chuck Serig discussed in Chapter XIII have a chance to start over again. Two of Chuck's children, four of his grandchildren, and nine of his great-grandchildren, still live in the Wheeling area. In thirty years, or fifty years, will some of his 2x or 3x great-grandchildren still be living in Wheeling, and for those who are, will these fourth and fifth cousins understand how they are related? Or will those fourth and fifth cousins just be some "other" Serigs to whom they think they are not related?

Serigs Currently in Wheeling Area - 2021			
Dillonvale			**Bethany**
Dean Serig (H)	**Rayland Yorkville**		Patricia McKeen (H)
Robert Serig (H)	Jonathan Nixon (A)		
Barbara Ries (A)	Julia Nixon (A)		
	Arielle Nixon (A)		
	Bridgeport		
St. Clairsville	Brian Habig (H)	**Wheeling**	
Markie Kaminsky (H)	Marjorie Lofton (A)	Linda Mann (H)	
Lindsey Mann (H)		Kerrie Kaminsky (H)	
Sally Muldoon (H)		Jessica Mann (H)	
		Morgan Mann (H)	
		Ronald Habig (H)	**Moundsville**
		Kevin Serig (A)	Joseph M. McMullen (H)
		Jake Wood (A)	Joseph N. McMullen (H)
		Stephanie Serig (A)	Jessica Rine (A)
		Morgan Diehl (A)	Isabella Rine (A)
		Mason Diehl (A)	Miley Rine (A)
		Amy Moses (A)	Jaxson Rine (A)
		Elijah Moses (A)	
(H) indicates Henry's line and (A) indicates Augustus' line			

Appendix – Serig Family Burials

Burial locations in Wheeling for the Serig family are summarized on the following pages. Those from the Henry line are in the Mount Wood, Greenwood, and Mount Calvary Cemeteries.

In the Mount Wood Cemetery, the earliest grave is Henry E. Serig's (1809 – 1851), and the most recent grave is Clotilda Serig's (1873 – 1968). In the Greenwood Cemetery, the earliest grave is Chester Bell's (1874 – 1912), and the most recent grave is Mary Emily Metzger's (nee McMullen, 1945 – 2018).

In the list of members of the Henry line buried in the Greenwood Cemetery, four are in bold. Those are the four grave markers that Amy asked about when she took her son Eli to ride his bike in the cemetery, starting this whole project. Two are George Serig (1871 – 1956) and his wife Maude Serig (nee Cotts, 1877 – 1923). George was Henry J. Serig's grandson. The other two are Charles Serig (1901 – 1981) and his wife, Wilma Serig (nee King, 1901 – 1983). Charles was George Serig's son.

Three members of the Henry line are buried in the Mount Calvary Cemetery. They are Harold Thomas Serig (1909 – 1952), his wife, Gertrude Serig (nee Foran, 1909 – 1982), and their daughter, Mary Ann Gray (nee Serig, 1940 – 2011).

Members of the Augustus line are located in the Mount Zion, Greenwood, and Seven Dolors Cemeteries. The earliest grave is that of Augustus Serig (1812 – 1862) who was buried in the Mount Zion Cemetery. Caroline Neutzling (nee Harding, 1868 – 1954) was the last member of the Augustus line buried at Mount Zion.

The first member of the Augustus line to be buried in the Greenwood Cemetery was Marjorie Woods (1919 – 1920). The last member of the Augustus line buried at Greenwood was Mary Elizabeth Ries (nee Burger, 1931 – 2017).

Two members of the Augustus line are buried in the Seven Dolors Cemetery. They are Charles "Chuck" Serig (1923 – 2003), and his wife, Ruth Serig (nee Klinkler, 1924 – 2007).

Greenwood Cemetery was the only cemetery used by both lines of the Serig family. Fifty-two family members are buried there, thirty-two from the Henry line and twenty from the Augustus line.

Members of the Henry Line of the Serig Family Buried in the Mount Wood Cemetery			
Last Name (Maiden)	**First Name**	**Birth**	**Death**
Serig	Henry E.	1809	1851
Serig	Lusetta	1839	1851
Serig	William	1842	1862
Serig	Leonora	1862	1871
Serig	Henry	1870	1871
Serig	Charles E.	1871	1872
Serig	Lusetta	1879	1879
Serig	Edward	1878	1879
Serig	Mary Christina	1865	1882
Serig	Ettie	1880	1883
Serig (Dipple)	Mary Christina	1813	1888
Serig	Christina L.	1875	1896
Serig	Henry J.	1836	1916
Serig	Albert	1845	1921
Serig	Frank	1875	1921
Serig	Louis August	1843	1923
Serig (Lewellen)	Sarah Anna	1848	1927
Serig	Leonora	1870	1928
Serig (Maser)	Louisa	1841	1928
Serig (Sykes)	Sarah Virginia	1849	1944
Serig	Elizabeth	1867	1961
Serig	Clotilda	1873	1968

<table>
<tr><td colspan="4">Members of the Henry Line
of the Serig Family
Buried in the Greenwood Cemetery</td></tr>
<tr><th>Last Name (Maiden)</th><th>First Name</th><th>Birth</th><th>Death</th></tr>
<tr><td>Bell</td><td>Chester Kemple</td><td>1874</td><td>1912</td></tr>
<tr><td>Serig (Cotts)</td><td>Maude</td><td>1877</td><td>1923</td></tr>
<tr><td>Schultze</td><td>August</td><td>1877</td><td>1924</td></tr>
<tr><td>Schultze (Wagner)</td><td>Madeline</td><td>1911</td><td>1947</td></tr>
<tr><td>Serig (Lynch)</td><td>Mary K</td><td>1888</td><td>1947</td></tr>
<tr><td>Serig</td><td>William</td><td>1868</td><td>1948</td></tr>
<tr><td>Serig (Lace)</td><td>Jessie Mae</td><td>1886</td><td>1948</td></tr>
<tr><td>Serig</td><td>Mary Christina</td><td>1869</td><td>1952</td></tr>
<tr><td>Serig</td><td>Mary Christina</td><td>1869</td><td>1952</td></tr>
<tr><td>Serig (Nightingale)</td><td>Martha</td><td>1872</td><td>1952</td></tr>
<tr><td>Serig</td><td>Harry</td><td>1883</td><td>1954</td></tr>
<tr><td>Serig</td><td>George</td><td>1871</td><td>1956</td></tr>
<tr><td>Bell (Serig)</td><td>Laura</td><td>1876</td><td>1963</td></tr>
<tr><td>Neer</td><td>Carl</td><td>1895</td><td>1964</td></tr>
<tr><td>Muldoon (Serig)</td><td>Mary Kathleen</td><td>1914</td><td>1965</td></tr>
<tr><td>Serig</td><td>Albert</td><td>1880</td><td>1965</td></tr>
<tr><td>Serig</td><td>Carl Henry</td><td>1884</td><td>1966</td></tr>
<tr><td>McMullen</td><td>John</td><td>1897</td><td>1968</td></tr>
<tr><td>Serig (Schultze)</td><td>Anna Mary</td><td>1880</td><td>1968</td></tr>
<tr><td>Serig</td><td>Sara</td><td>1878</td><td>1970</td></tr>
<tr><td>Serig (Fiveash)</td><td>Vivian Christine</td><td>1912</td><td>1975</td></tr>
<tr><td>Serig (Yeager)</td><td>Mary</td><td>1924</td><td>1975</td></tr>
</table>

Serig	Cora	1888	1979
Serig	**Charles Louis**	**1901**	**1981**
Serig (King)	**Wilma**	**1900**	**1983**
McMullen (Serig)	Anna Catherine	1911	1985
Schultze	Clarence	1906	1985
Serig	Howard William	1901	1989
Neer (Serig)	Virginia May	1899	1991
Muldoon	Robert	1916	1996
Serig	John William	1917	2004
Metzger (McMullen)	Mary Emily	1945	2018

Members of the Henry Line of the Serig Family Buried in the Mount Calvary Cemetery			
Last Name (Maiden)	**First Name**	**Birth**	**Death**
Serig	Harold Thomas	1909	1952
Serig (Foran)	Gertrude	1909	1982
Gray (Serig)	Mary Ann	1940	2011

Members of the Augustus Line of the Serig Family Buried in the Mount Zion Cemetery

Last Name (Maiden)	First Name	Birth	Death
Serig	Augustus	1812	1862
Harding	Louis	1840	1869
Serig	George	1878	1880
Neutzling	Ella	1884	1886
?	Sophia Elizabeth	1820	1891
Harding (Serig)	Matilda	1845	1892
Serig	Guy	1883	1901
Neutzling	Peter	1862	1927
Neutzling (Harding)	Caroline	1868	1954

Members of the Augustus Line of the Serig Family Buried in the Greenwood Cemetery

Last Name (Maiden)	First Name	Birth	Death
Woods	Marjorie	1919	1920
Baker (Serig)	Merle	1899	1923
Serig	Louis Albert	1922	1923
Serig (Eberling)	Amelia	1874	1923
Moore	John	1863	1933
Serig (Ward)	Loma	1901	1938
Klinkler	George August	1860	1942
Moore (Harding)	Elizabeth	1864	1943

Klinkler (Zimmer)	Hannah	1863	1946
Serig	Louis August	1871	1946
Ries	Ellen Sue	1953	1953
Ries (Cecil)	Norma Jeanne	1932	1955
Woods	Ralph	1890	1955
Klinkler (Friedhof)	Katharine	1896	1961
Woods (Moore)	Carrie	1891	1981
Klinkler	Albert George	1895	1994
Ries	Glenn Robert	1928	2007
Flanders (Dueker)	Elizabeth Jane	1928	2012
Flanders	Albert Charles	1919	2015
Ries (Burger)	Mary Elizabeth	1931	2017

Members of the Augustus Line of the Serig Family Buried in the Seven Dolors Cemetery			
Last Name (Maiden)	**First Name**	**Birth**	**Death**
Serig	Charles	1923	2003
Serig (Klinkler)	Ruth	1924	2007